D0202777

THE ROAD TO RUIN

THOMAS HOLCROFT

The Road to Ruin

Edited by

RUTH I. ALDRICH

UNIVERSITY OF NEBRASKA PRESS · LINCOLN

Contents

List of Abbreviations

MS	Manuscript of *The Road to Ruin*, Larpent Collection, Huntington Library.
Q1	First Quarto, 1792.
Q2	Second Quarto, 1792.
Q3	Third Quarto, 1792.
Q4	Fourth Quarto, 1792.
Q5	Fifth Quarto, 1792.
Q6	Sixth Quarto, 1792.
Q9	Ninth Quarto, 1792.
Q10	Tenth Quarto, 1792.
Q11	Eleventh Quarto, 1792.
Q12	"New Edition," 1802.
Inch.	Mrs. Elizabeth Inchbald. *The British Theatre*. London, 1824.
Ox.	W. Oxberry. *The New English Drama*. London, 1819.
DNB	*Dictionary of National Biography*.
OED	*Oxford English Dictionary*.
om.	omitted

Introduction

The Road to Ruin (entitled on the manuscript *The City Prodigals or The Widow Bewitched*) was first produced at Covent Garden on Saturday, February 18, 1792, and was received with acclaim. During the season it ran for thirty-seven performances, one of which was attended by King George III and Queen Charlotte, and with two exceptions it formed the bill for each performance at Covent Garden from February 18 through March 24. On the opening night the receipts were just over £231; on the third evening, Holcroft's benefit night, they were almost £218, and they continued high. On April 30, for example, they were nearly £208 compared to £102 for *The Rivals* on May 2; on May 14 they were £239 while *The Comedy of Errors* on May 18 and *Cymbeline* on May 19 drew £104 each.

On September 17, 1792, *The Road to Ruin* opened the fall season of the new Covent Garden Theatre, which had been almost entirely rebuilt during the summer. To regain the cost of the remodeling, the shilling gallery was abolished, with such consequent pandemonium on the first night that the first two acts of the play had to be panto-mimed since they could not be heard. (On September 20 an announcement that the shilling price would be reinstated ended the disturbances.) In the summer of 1792, between the Covent Garden seasons, the comedy was given in Ireland in Cork, Newry, and Waterford, and the following fall and winter in Wexford and Derry.[1]

The play appeared on the stage constantly for many years; Hazlitt could say of it that it carried Holcroft's fame to every place in England where there was a playhouse.[2] Holcroft himself reported in his diary in 1798 that the only theaters in Great Britain in which the play had not been acted fifty times were Drury Lane (where it was first given in June, 1803), the Haymarket, and the Opera House,

[1] William Smith Clark, *The Irish Stage in the County Towns* (Oxford, 1965), pp. 133, 315.
[2] William Hazlitt, *Memoirs of the Late Thomas Holcroft*, in *Complete Works*, ed. P. P. Howe, III (London, 1932), 121.

these three coming under the still-existent Licensing Act.[3] It remained popular in England for nearly a hundred and fifty years, having London revivals in 1873 (when it ran for 118 nights), in 1915, and in 1937.

In the United States the drama was performed for the first time on February 8, 1793, at the John Street Theatre, New York, and it continued to be acted as a favorite of stock companies for a century, Mrs. John Drew playing the Widow Warren in New York on January 8, 1894, to a crowded house, and on January 15, 1894, when her grandson Lionel Barrymore acted a footman. In 1823 the part of Goldfinch was the first New York role taken by Charles Mathews, the English actor; the *Post* reported: "The house overflowed so much and so early that the manager was called forward at half past six and entreated to order the door of the pit to be shut against any further entrance, which was accordingly done."[4] Mathews' final performance before leaving the United States was again as Goldfinch, and the house once more was crowded to overflowing. Joseph Jefferson, the celebrated American comedian, also played Goldfinch and was seen in the role by Washington Irving.

At the time of the original production, Thomas Holcroft was a self-educated man of forty-six who had already written novels, plays, and theatrical criticism which anticipated the later dramatic essays of Hunt and Hazlitt; he had also published translations and acted minor parts in Dublin under Charles Macklin, in the provinces with the Kembles' troupe, and in London. He had been a friend of William Godwin for some six years and knew Thomas Paine, James Mackintosh, and Mary Wollstonecraft, but his indictment for high treason and the radical reputation which was to affect the reception of his later plays were yet in the future.

Two of the opening night actors, William Thomas Lewis (1748?–1811), who was also acting manager of Covent Garden Theatre for twenty-one years, and Joseph Munden (1758–1832) became famous for their playing of the parts of Goldfinch and Old Dornton. The manuscript of the play shows John Quick in the role of Old Dornton and Munden as Silky, and according to George Daniels Munden only reluctantly changed parts with Quick. Of Munden, Charles Lamb commented that as Dornton he could "diffuse a glow of

[3] *Memoirs*, p. 193.

[4] George C. D. Odell, *Annals of the New York Stage*, III (New York, 1928), 49.

sentiment which has made the pulse of a crowded theatre beat like that of one man."[5] However, Leigh Hunt preferred the acting of William Dowton (1764–1851), who was the first Old Dornton at Drury Lane Theatre (1803) and who was still playing the role in 1824. Hunt, who regarded Dowton as unsurpassable as Sir Anthony Absolute, a somewhat similar type, said that Dowton had "proved himself superior not only to the face-making Munden, but perhaps to any actor in the recollection of the present time," continuing: "Munden, who really has a considerable share of feeling, injures his Dornton, as he does all his characters, with the most preposterous buffoonery: he hurts alike his rage and his tenderness, his violent, his soft, and his comic expression with this studious farce, because he renders it evident to the whole house that he is not sufficiently occupied with himself to give a good portrait of himself, or rather, perhaps, that he is too much occupied with himself to give a good portrait of his author's personage."[6]

The *Monthly Review* credited the pleasure caused by the character of Goldfinch to the acting of William Lewis, which was also praised by Hazlitt.

Of the remaining original performers, Macready (who played Mr. Williams, the hosier) was the father of the famous actor William Charles Macready. Joseph George Holman (1764–1817), who played Harry Dornton, first appeared at Covent Garden in 1784 as Romeo, when he was twenty. He is said to have been strikingly handsome, elegant, animated, and graceful, with an expressive countenance; Lamb remarks on his "bright glittering teeth."[7] John Quick (1748–1831), the original Silky, is said to have been the favorite actor of George III, which may account for the attendance of the King and Queen at the performance on March 15, 1792. Lamb mentions "little Quick . . . with his squeak like a Bart'lemew fiddle," and refers to George Harley, who played Milford, as Holman's rival.[8] According to the manuscript Milford was originally to have been given by William Farren; the substitution is perhaps explained by John

[5] Charles Lamb, "On the Acting of Munden," in *The Works of Charles and Mary Lamb*, ed. E. V. Lucas, II (London, 1903), 149.

[6] Leigh Hunt, *Dramatic Essays*, ed. William Archer and Robert W. Lowe (London, 1894), pp. 63–64.

[7] Charles Lamb, "The Old Actors," in *The Works of Charles and Mary Lamb*, ed. E. V. Lucas, II (London, 1903), 294.

[8] *Ibid.*

Genest's comment that by 1795 Farren had grown "rather too fat" for young men.[9] The prologue was probably spoken by John Fawcett (1768–1837) a comedian, whose greatest successes came after 1797.

Of the three important women's parts, Mrs. Isabella Mattocks (1746–1826) played the Widow Warren and delivered the epilogue. According to Genest, she was an excellent epilogue speaker; her epilogues are also referred to in "Anthony Pasquin's" (John Williams) *The Children of Thespis*, 1786. Lamb calls her "the sensiblest of viragos," though this does not fully describe the hearty vulgarity she must have given to the Widow. The role of Jenny was taken by Mrs. Sarah Harlowe (1765–1852), who had made her first appearance at Covent Garden in November, 1791, and who was in later years to play the Widow Warren. Leigh Hunt found her commendable in parts calling for her scolding and chambermaid airs. The first Sophia was Elizabeth Brunton Merry (1769–1808), who in August, 1791, had married Robert Merry of Della Cruscan fame. She withdrew from Covent Garden in the spring of 1792 either because of a quarrel with the management or the objections of her husband's family, and after 1796 she lived in the United States, where she became well known as manager and actress. At the time she played Sophia she was twenty-three. (When Mrs. Elizabeth Jordan played Sophia with Dowton in 1803, she was forty-one.) Genest says that her features were "neither delicate nor expressive, but her voice was sonorous, flexible, and sweetly melodious—her deportment was graceful, and her action nicely and judiciously adapted to the situation—her enunciation was animated—she caught the fire of her author, and was guided by a feeling heart."[10] Fanny Kelly, the friend of Lamb, was also one of the Sophias of the early part of the century.

Interesting glimpses of the appearance of the characters are given in some of the editions of *The Road to Ruin*. Holcroft mentions the Widow's "fantastic girlish morning dress." Oxberry (1819) describes it as spangled and trimmed with black, with a second dress of white satin trimmed with silver and spangled drapery; his Sophia wears a white frock with a black sash. Cumberland's *British Theatre*, 1829, preserves Sophia's white muslin, but gives her pink trimming, and the Widow Warren is again in white satin—one dress trimmed with green, and one with a profusion of gold spangles worn with a white,

---

[9] John Genest, *Some Account of the English Stage*, VII (Bath, 1832), 220.
[10] *Ibid.*, p. 75.

gold-spangled satin turban with white plumes. By 1829 the clothes worn by Old Dornton and Sulky are termed old-fashioned. Gold-finch's costume is set with his entrance in 1792; both Oxberry and Cumberland describe the same outfit: scarlet frock coat, buff waistcoat, white cord breeches, top-boots.

Of the early critics, the *Monthly Review* for March, 1792, granted the comedy a "respectable rank among the new productions," but regarded it as a "modern play" of transient popularity and found the plot too improbable. The *Analytical Review* in July, 1792, quoted at some length from the play and gave it a very brief critical comment (attributed by Elbridge Colby to Mary Wollstonecraft)[11] mentioning an understanding of stage effect, touches of both fustian and nature, the "flippant dialogue of artificial life," and imperfect sketches of passion. Also in July, 1792, the *English Review* quoted from the play at length, summarized the remainder of the plot, and said that the comedy, though amusing in an inferior degree, made a moral point, and that the plot and ingenious characters would add to Holcroft's reputation.

When *The Road to Ruin* appeared in drama collections, Hazlitt, Mrs. Inchbald, and George Daniels contributed introductions. In her collection of 1808 (reprinted in 1824), Mrs. Inchbald placed it among the most successful of modern plays, with skill in the dialogue and excellent dramatic technique. However, she considered the character of Sophia too foolish for a girl of seventeen. Hazlitt gave the work high praise both in the discussion in his edition of Holcroft's *Memoirs* and in his introduction to Oxberry's reprint. In the *Memoirs* he states: "The story never stagnates for a moment; the whole is full, crowded, and the wonder seems to be how so many incidents, so regularly connected, and so clearly explained, can be brought together in so small a compass. At the same time, the hurry of events, and the intricacy of the plot, do not interfere with the unfolding of the characters, or the forcible expression of the passions."[12] His comments in "The Comic Writers of the Last Century" and in the introduction to Oxberry's reprint are somewhat less enthusiastic; he approves the character of Old Dornton, the relationship between Dornton and his son, and sees Goldfinch as the forerunner of a race of impertinent

[11] William Hazlitt, *The Life of Thomas Holcroft*, ed. Elbridge Colby, I (London, 1925), 293 n.
[12] *Memoirs*, p. 124.

dramatic heroes, but like Mrs. Inchbald he thinks Sophia an insipid failure. George Daniels, in introductory remarks to the reprint in Cumberland's *British Theatre*, 1829, is more restrained: "The plot is natural and interesting, and the language flows in an easy and colloquial style. The sentiments are those of truth and virtue—and the whole is well seasoned with humor." While Daniels admits that Goldfinch is amusing on the stage, his interpretation of the gambler's personality, "a vulgar rake, gross and illiterate—without mind or manners," contradicts that of Hazlitt. Finally, Mary Shelley declared that Holcroft's comedy "will always maintain its position on the English stage, so long as there are actors who can fitly represent its leading characters."[13]

The critics of the revivals have not been as kind. To the reviewer for the *Athenaeum*, November, 1873, *The Road to Ruin* was "an indifferent piece," although he admitted that the scenes were "tolerably ingenious," and that the audience responded to the play, leading him to suppose that the performance would prove a lasting success. In March of the war year 1915 the *Nation* dismissed the comedy as "a machine-made play, cleverly put together from traditional types and traditional situations" (disagreeing with the critics of Holcroft's own day who found it modern). Finally, judging the revival of February, 1937, the *Spectator* considered it only a period play, based on familiar situations, but added that its conventional plot is "neatly worked out, that the dialogue is for its time remarkably smooth and natural, and that the characters are admirably built."

That the play uses familiar material (such as the character-revealing names and the scene of mistaken identity) is clear to us; it was perhaps not as clear to the readers and audiences of the time, although Hazlitt finds Harry Dornton "something like" Charles Surface of Sheridan's *The School for Scandal*,[14] and the *Monthly Review* suggests that Goldfinch derives from Squire Groom of Charles Macklin's *Love à la Mode* (1759). If the comedy uses types, however, they are well diversified. Sophia, criticized for her naiveté and foolishness, is actually clearly identified in the play as the hoyden known in Restoration and eighteenth-century drama; the Widow Warren is the often seen matrimonially minded older woman; Old

[13] C. Kegan Paul, *William Godwin: His Friends and Contemporaries*, I (London, 1876), 26.

[14] *Memoirs*, p. 123.

Dornton is the typical gruff but affectionate father; Silky is the sly, avaricious usurer. But the character of Goldfinch, a city man whose father rose from the lower class, is new; he exhibits the lack of taste and love of low company which reappears in the minor characters of much Victorian fiction (he has been hailed as a forerunner of Jingle in *Pickwick Papers*). Hazlitt says: "The character of Goldfinch, though not the principal character, was undoubtedly that which contributed most to the popularity of the piece. Nine persons out of ten who went to see the Road to Ruin, went for the sake of seeing Goldfinch; . . . nothing can exceed the life, the spirit, the extreme volubility, the restless animation, which Mr. Holcroft has thrown into this character." [15] Though the redemption of a carefree young man-about-town is a well-worn subject, as is the conflict between love and honor or filial affection, even the more critical reviewers admitted that in spite of some improbabilities the plot moves rapidly and is deftly held together with hints and foreshadowings.

The play does exhibit some of Holcroft's liberal tendencies. Its prologue is not yet out of date (Allardyce Nicoll said of it that few authors, even when jesting, dared to be so explicit),[16] while the scene with the hosier, actually irrelevant to the plot, restates the prologue's emphasis on the equality of men. There are terse suggestions of social wrongs, usually in connection with the Widow Warren, such as her unfeeling treatment of Mrs. Ledger and of Milford. Duelling is attacked in a rather traditional way in the quarrel between Harry Dornton and Milford.

Although the theme of the play is stated in the last scene as the dangers of the undiscriminating but generous heart, the true emphasis is on money—an indication of the rising status of the middle class and the influence of the new industrial world. Whether this emphasis was a part of Holcroft's liberalism, a reflection of his own rise in the world, or a conscious perception of the economic and social changes stirring in England, Holcroft suggests the importance of the commercial and mercantile class in the newly rich Goldfinch, the former clerk Sulky, and the usurer Silky who had faced a debtor's prison. The resolution of the plot provides wealth as well as happiness for the principal characters: Harry Dornton is fortunate enough to

[15] *Memoirs*, p. 122.

[16] Allardyce Nicoll, *A History of English Drama 1660–1900*, III (Cambridge, 1961), 55.

win not merely the prize of love, but the fortune he sought in the widow's hand, for Sophia is the heiress of her stepfather; Sulky is the sole inheritor of a wealthy uncle; both Harry Dornton's and Milford's creditors will be paid in full; and the bank does not fail. The minor characters likewise are concerned with money: Mrs. Ledger appears only to ask for aid, the group of tradesmen (with one exception) charge as much as they dare, and Jenny takes whatever may be obtained in the way of money or gifts. The core of the plot is the potential failure of the firm and the disposal of the £150,000 legacy, while the bank office and Silky's office, a "room of business" with ledger, inkstand, letter-files, provide the setting for several scenes. And we find in the play no lords or ladies, no aristocratic background, but the people of the day. It was perhaps because of this emphasis on money that the audience so admired the carefree Goldfinch who will not turn to trade and who perhaps will win in the next Newmarket races.

This edition of *The Road to Ruin* is the first since 1883, and is the first with textual and explanatory notes. The initial publication of the play came shortly after the first stage production, when the *Universal Magazine* announced *The Road to Ruin* as a new publication in February, 1792, and the demand for the play is indicated by the eleven quarto editions which were printed in that year. In addition, a Dublin edition appeared in 1792, and Elbridge Colby lists a New York edition for the same year. In 1802 a "New Edition" was published, lacking the prologue and epilogue, printing without quotation marks the lines omitted in representation, and filled with minor variations of punctuation and spelling as well as many printing errors. It also made slight changes in the stage directions. The first reprint in a dramatic collection was that of Mrs. Inchbald, *The British Theatre*, 1808. Many other editions exist; one is a reprint of Mrs. Inchbald's edition, printed in Calcutta—an indication of the interests and attitudes of the British residents. The play has been translated into at least three languages.

The manuscript of *The Road to Ruin* is in the Larpent Collection of the Henry E. Huntington Library and Art Gallery, San Marino, California. Its original title, *The City Prodigals or The Widow Bewitched*, stresses the plot. A large number of lines and fairly long sections of scenes were cancelled from the manuscript; these cancellations, such as that of a long catechistic questioning by Jenny concerning Sophia's life in the country, invariably show Holcroft's knowledge of stage technique and audience interest. Treatment of the Widow Warren seems to have given Holcroft the most trouble; a number of her lines retained in the first edition were not presented on the stage, while Harry's proposal to her (IV.i) went through a great deal of rewriting, as did the scenes (V.i) in which this match is broken off and Goldfinch accepted. Some speeches between Milford and Harry, and Milford or Harry and Goldfinch, were cancelled apparently because they were repetitive. The scene in which Silky learns of Milford's arrest was moved from Act III to Act II for the sake of more rapid action.

The text used in this edition is that of Q1. The textual notes show the major variations from Q1 of the manuscript, of eight of the remaining ten quartos of 1792 (lacking the seventh and eighth editions), of the "New Edition" of 1802, and of the printings in 1824 by Mrs. Inchbald ("from the promptbook") and in 1819 by William Oxberry, himself an actor, whom Hazlitt refers to as "of a strong rather than of a pleasant comic vein." The 1824 edition by Mrs. Inchbald was selected rather than that of 1808 since the later edition is closer to Q1, while that of 1808 in several cases resembles the "New Edition." All of the omissions made by Mrs. Inchbald and by Oxberry from Q1 are listed, as are lines appearing in Q1 which do not appear or which are cancelled in the manuscript, and lines which are in the manuscript but not in Q1.

Of the eleven editions of 1792 which are available, it is clear that Q1 is the basis for the rest, although there are minor variations between all of them except possibly between Q2 and Q3. It is also clear that Q1, Q2, and Q3 have strong resemblances, as do Q5 and Q6, and Q9, Q10, and Q11.

Textual variations are ordinarily indicated only when they are major variations or when they appear in more than one edition. Omission of a siglum after the bracket indicates that the reading of the edition in question agrees with that of the text. Spelling has in general been altered to bring it into accord with modern practice, and punctuation has also been silently altered or added, though in general exclamation marks have been retained as they were in the original. An appendix lists the lines which were omitted in representation and set off by quotation marks in the eleven quartos of 1792.

I am indebted to many librarians and scholars for assistance in locating editions and providing explanatory material, and I wish to express particular gratitude to The Huntington Library, San Marino, California, for their permission to use and reproduce the manuscript copy of *The Road to Ruin* in the Larpent Collection (LA 935).

RUTH I. ALDRICH

University of Wisconsin–Milwaukee

Bibliography

Colby, Elbridge. *A Bibliography of Thomas Holcroft*. The New York Public Library, 1922.

Colby, Elbridge. "Financial Accounts of Holcroft's Plays," *Notes and Queries*, CXLVI (1924), 60–63.

Genest, John. *Some Account of the English Stage*. 10 vols. Bath, 1832.

Hazlitt, William. "Comic Writers of the Last Century," in *Complete Works*, ed. P. P. Howe. Vol. VI (London, 1931), 149–168.

Hazlitt, William. *The Life of Thomas Holcroft*, ed. Elbridge Colby. 2 vols. London, 1925.

Hazlitt, William. *Memoirs of the Late Thomas Holcroft*, in *Complete Works*, ed. P. P. Howe. Vol. III, London, 1932.

Hazlitt, William. "Prefatory Remarks to Oxberry's New English Drama," in *Complete Works*, ed. P. P. Howe. Vol. IX (London, 1932), 87–88.

Holcroft, Thomas. *The Road to Ruin*, in Mrs. Elizabeth Inchbald's *The British Theatre*. Vol. XXIV, London, 1824.

Holcroft, Thomas. *The Road to Ruin*, in W. Oxberry's *The New English Drama*. Vol. VII, London, 1819.

Odell, George C. D. *Annals of the New York Stage*. 15 vols. New York, 1949.

Paul, C. Kegan. *William Godwin: His Friends and Contemporaries*. 2 vols. London, 1876.

THE ROAD TO RUIN

PROLOGUE

Spoken by Mr. Fawcett

Enter, driving a boy across the stage.

Away! 'Sblood! Run for the author! We can do nothing till
    he appears.
Tell him in less than five minutes we shall have the house
    about our ears!

To the audience.

Oh, sirs! The prompter has mislaid the prologue, and we are
    all amort.
I suppose our friends above yonder will soon be making
    pretty sport!
For pity's sake, suffer us to go on without it. —Good, dear
    sirs, do!   5
'Twas most abominably dull. —Zounds! There stands the
    writer. Well! It's very true.
One of our te-tum-ti heroes was to have spoken it, who
    measure out nonsense by the yard;
And our chief hope was you'd make too much noise for it to
    be heard.
The author had mounted on the stilts of oratory and
    elocution:
Not but he had a smart touch or two, about Poland, France,
    and the—the revolution;   10
Telling us that Frenchman, and Polishman, and every man
    is our brother:
And that all men, ay, even poor Negro men, have a right to
    be free, one as well as another!
Freedom at length, said he, like a torrent is spreading and
    swelling,
To sweep away pride and reach the most miserable
    dwelling;

*Prologue om. Q*12, *Inch.*

---

3. *amort*] confounded.

To ease, happiness, art, science, wit, and genius to give
    birth;   15
Ay, to fertilize a world, and renovate old earth!

    Thus he went on, not mentioning a word about the play;
For he says prologues are blots, which ought to be wiped
    away;
A Gothic practice, and, in spite of precedent, not the better
    for being old;
For, if we tell any part of the plot, it then becomes a tale
    twice told;   20
And such twice telling can rarely once excite our wonder:
Ergo, he that says nothing is least likely to blunder.
Since therefore prologues are bad things at best, pray, my
    good friends,
Never mind the want of one, but live in hopes the play will
    make amends.

DRAMATIS PERSONAE

MR. DORNTON   *Mr. Munden*
HARRY DORNTON   *Mr. Holman*
MR. SULKY   *Mr. Wilson*
MR. SILKY   *Mr. Quick*
GOLDFINCH   *Mr. Lewis*
MR. MILFORD   *Mr. Harley*
MR. SMITH   *Mr. Powell*
HOSIER   *Mr. Macready*
SHERIFF'S OFFICER   *Mr. Thompson*
JACOB   *Mr. Rees*
WAITER
CLERKS
SERVANTS
POSTILLIONS
TRADESMEN
TENNIS MARKERS, &c.

MRS. WARREN   *Mrs. Mattocks*
SOPHIA   *Mrs. Merry*
JENNY   *Mrs. Harlowe*
MRS. LEDGER   *Mrs. Powell*
MILLINER
MANTEAUMAKER

Scene, *London*. Time not twenty-four hours.

The Road to Ruin
A Comedy

ACT I

[I.i] *The house of Dornton.*
Mr. Dornton alone.

DORNTON.

Past two o'clock and not yet returned! Well, well! It's my
own fault! —Mr. Smith!

Enter Mr. Smith.

MR. SMITH.

Sir.

DORNTON.

Is Mr. Sulky come in?

MR. SMITH.

No, sir.   5

DORNTON.

Are you sure Harry Dornton said he should return tonight?

MR. SMITH.

Yes, sir.

DORNTON.

And you don't know where he is gone?

MR. SMITH.

He did not tell me, sir.

DORNTON (*angrily*).

I ask if you know!   10

MR. SMITH.

I believe to Newmarket, sir.

The Road to Ruin: A Comedy]   COMEDY *MS;* A COMEDY
THE CITY PRODIGALS: A   *om. Q12, Inch., Ox.*

11. *Newmarket*] a town east of Cambridge where horse races are held.

DORNTON.

> You always believe the worst! —I'll sit up no longer. Tell the
> servants to go to bed. And do you hear, should he apply to
> you for money, don't let him have a guinea.

MR. SMITH.

> Very well, sir. 15

DORNTON.

> I have done with him; he is henceforth no son of mine! Let
> him starve!

MR. SMITH.

> He acts very improperly, sir, indeed.

DORNTON (*alarmed*).

> Improperly! How? What does he do?

MR. SMITH.

> Sir! 20

DORNTON.

> Have you heard anything of——?

MR. SMITH (*confused*).

> No—no, sir—nothing—nothing but what you yourself tell me.

DORNTON.

> Then how do you know he has acted improperly?

MR. SMITH.

> He is certainly a very good-hearted young gentleman, sir.

DORNTON.

> Good-hearted! How dare you make such an assertion? 25

MR. SMITH.

> Sir!

DORNTON.

> How dare you, Mr. Smith, insult me so? Is not his gaming
> notorious; his racing, driving, riding, and associating with
> knaves, fools, debauchees, and blacklegs?

MR. SMITH.

> Upon my word, sir—I— 30

DORNTON.

> But it's over! His name has this very day been struck out of
> the firm! Let his drafts be returned. It's all ended! (*Passion-
> ately.*)   And, observe, not a guinea! If you lend him any

---

29. *blacklegs*] swindlers and gamblers, perhaps so called from their
appearance usually in boots.

32. *drafts*] bills of exchange; orders for money payable.

yourself I'll not pay you. I'll no longer be a fond doting
father! (*With great passion.*) Therefore take warning! Take   35
warning, I say! Be his distress what it will, not a guinea!
Though you should hereafter see him begging, starving in
the streets, not so much as the loan or the gift of a single
guinea!

MR. SMITH.

I shall be careful to observe your orders, sir.   40

DORNTON (*terror*).

Sir! Why, would you see him starve? Would you see him
starve and not lend him a guinea? Would you, sir? Would
you?

MR. SMITH.

Sir! Certainly not, except in obedience to your orders!

DORNTON (*amazement and compassion*).

And could any orders justify your seeing a poor unfortunate   45
youth, rejected by his father, abandoned by his friends,
starving to death?

MR. SMITH.

There is no danger of that, sir.

DORNTON.

I tell you the thing shall happen! He shall starve to death!
(*Horror at the supposition.*)   I'll never look on him more as a   50
son of mine; and I am very certain, when I have forsaken
him, all the world will forsake him too.   (*Almost in tears.*)
Yes, yes! He is born to be a poor wretched outcast!

MR. SMITH.

I hope, sir, he still will make a fine man.

DORNTON.

Will? —There is not a finer, handsomer, nobler looking   55
youth in the kingdom; no, not in the world!

MR. SMITH.

I mean a worthy good man, sir.

DORNTON.

How can you mean any such thing? The company he keeps
would corrupt a saint.

MR. SMITH.

Sir, if you will only tell me what your pleasure is, I will   60
endeavor to act like a faithful servant.

55. Will?] Will! *Q12, Inch., Ox.*

DORNTON (*takes his hand*).

I know you are a faithful servant, Mr. Smith. I know you
are. But you—you are not a father.

Enter Mr. Sulky, *and* Mr. Smith *goes off.*

Well, Mr. Sulky, have you heard anything of him?

SULKY.

Yes.   65

DORNTON (*excessively impatient*).

And, hey—? Anything consoling, anything good?

SULKY.

No.

DORNTON.

No? No, say you! Where is he? What is he about?

SULKY.

I don't know.

DORNTON.

Don't—? You love to torture me, sir! You love to torture   70
me.

SULKY.

Humph.

DORNTON.

For heaven's sake tell me what you have heard!

SULKY.

I love to torture you.

DORNTON.

Put me out of my pain! If you are not a tiger, put me out of   75
my pain!

SULKY (*reluctantly drawing a newspaper out of his pocket*).

There; read!

DORNTON.

Dead!

SULKY.

Worse.

DORNTON.

Mercy defend me! Where? What?   80

SULKY.

The first paragraph in the postscript: the beginning line in
capitals.

DORNTON (*reads*).

"The junior partner of the great banking house, not a mile

from the Post Office, has again been touched at Newmarket,
for upward of a thousand pounds." *(Pause.)* It can't be!   85

SULKY.

Humph.

DORNTON.

Why, can it?

SULKY.

Yes.

DORNTON.

How do you know? What proof have you that this is not a
lie?   90

SULKY.

His own handwriting.

DORNTON.

How!

SULKY.

Bills at three days' sight to the full amount have already been
presented.

DORNTON.

And accepted?   95

SULKY.

Yes.

DORNTON.

But! —Why! —Were you mad, Mr. Sulky? Were you mad?

SULKY.

I soon shall be.

DORNTON.

Is not his name struck off the firm?

SULKY.

They were dated two days before.   100

DORNTON.

The credit of my house begins to totter!

SULKY.

Well it may!

DORNTON.

What the effect of such a paragraph may be I cannot tell!

SULKY.

I can. Ruin.

DORNTON.

Are you serious, sir?   105

SULKY.

I am not inclined to laugh. A run against the house, stoppage, disgrace, bankruptcy.

DORNTON.

Really, Mr. Sulky, you—

SULKY.

Yes, I know I offend. I was bred in your house, you used me tenderly, I served you faithfully, and you admitted me a 110 partner. Don't think I care for myself. No. I can sit at the desk again. But you! You! First man of the first commercial city on earth, your name in the *Gazette*? Were it mine only I would laugh at it. What am I? Who cares for me?

DORNTON.

Where is the vile——?   115

SULKY.

Who can tell? With his lords and his ladies, his court friends and his Newmarket friends, his women of wit and his men of soul, his bluestockings and his blacklegs!

DORNTON (*calling*).

Mr. Smith! Thomas! William!

Enter Mr. Smith.

Call all the servants together, Mr. Smith; clerks, footmen, 120 maids, every soul! Tell them their young master is a scoundrel!

MR. SMITH.

Very well, sir.

DORNTON (*his anger recurring*).

Sir? —Bid them shut the door in his face! I'll turn the first away that lets him set foot in this house ever again!   125

MR. SMITH.

Very well, sir.

DORNTON.

Very well, sir? Damn your very well, sir! I tell you it is not

---

115–118. Where ... blacklegs]   116–118. Who ... blacklegs] *om.*
cancelled MS; om. Inch.   *Ox.*

---

113. *Gazette*] the *London Gazette*, published twice a week, and containing among other notices the names of bankrupts (*OED*).
118. *bluestockings*] women affecting literary tastes.

very well, sir. He shall starve, die, rot in the street! Is that
very well, sir?   *Exeunt* Mr. Dornton *and* Mr. Smith.

SULKY.

Has a noble heart. A fond father's heart. The boy was a fine 130
youth. But he spoiled him; and now he quarrels with himself
and all the world, because he hates his own folly.

Distant knocking heard at the street door.

So! Here is the youth returned.   *Knocking again.*

Enter Mr. Dornton, *followed by* Servants.

DORNTON.

Don't stir! On your lives, don't go to the door! Are the bolts
and locks all fastened?   135

SERVANTS.

All, sir.   *Knocking.*

DORNTON.

Don't mind his knocking! Go to bed every soul of you
instantly, and fall fast asleep! —He shall starve in the streets!
(*Knocking again.*)   Fetch me my blunderbuss! Make haste!

Exeunt.

[I.ii]   *Scene changes to the street before the door.*
            Harry Dornton, Milford, *and* Postillions.

POSTILLION.

We smoked along, your honor!

HARRY (*knocks*).

I know you did. Had you been less free with your whip you
would have been half a crown richer. Your next step should
be to turn drummers, and handle the cat o' nine tails.

POSTILLION.

It is very late, your honor!   5

HARRY (*knocks*).

Be gone! I'll give you no more.   *Exeunt* Postillions.

130. Has a] He has a *Q12, Inch., Ox.*   the richer *Q12;* a crown the richer
[I.ii]   *Ox.*
3. half a crown richer] half a crown

[I.ii]
4. *drummers*] The drummer also administered lashings.

DORNTON (*throwing up the sash and presenting the blunderbuss,* Mr. Sulky *behind*).

Knock again, you scoundrel, and you shall have the full contents loaded to the muzzle, rascal!

HARRY.

So! I suspected dad was in his tantarums.

MILFORD.

You have given him some cause.   10

HARRY.

Very true. (*To his father.*)   Consider, my dear sir, the consequences of lying out all night!

DORNTON.

Begone, villain!

HARRY.

Bad women, sir; damps, night air!

DORNTON.

Will you be gone?   15

HARRY.

Watch-houses, pickpockets, cutthroats!

SULKY.

Come, come, sir.   *Shutting down the window.*

MILFORD.

We shall not get in.

HARRY.

Pshaw! How little do you know of my father! The door will open in less than fifteen seconds.   20

MILFORD.

Done, for a hundred!

HARRY.

Done, done!

They take out their watches and the door opens.

I knew you were had; double or quits we find the cloth laid and supper on the table.

---

9. *tantarums*] tantrums.

16. *Watch-houses*] "a house used as a station for municipal night-watch-men, in which the chief constable of the night sits to receive and detain in custody till the morning any disorderly persons brought in by the watch-men" (*OED*).

MILFORD.

No, it won't do.   *Exeunt into the house.*

[I.iii]   *Scene changes to the former apartment.*
              Enter Harry Dornton, Milford, *and* Footman.

FOOTMAN.

My old master is in a bitter passion, sir.

HARRY.

I know it.

FOOTMAN.

He is gone down to turn the servant out of doors that let
you in.

HARRY.

Is he? Then go you and let your fellow servant in again.

FOOTMAN.

I dare not, sir.

HARRY.

Then I must.   *Exi*

FOOTMAN.

He enquired who was with my young master.

MILFORD.

Well!

FOOTMAN.

And when he heard it was you, sir, he was ten times more   10
furious.   *Exit* Footman.

              Re-enter Harry Dornton.

HARRY.

All's well that ends well. This has been a cursed losing
voyage, Milford!

MILFORD.

I am a hundred and fifty in.

HARRY.

And I ten thousand out!   15

[I.iii]   HARRY. Oh, no! We must first
1. bitter] terrible *MS*.   scold, curse, kiss and good night!
15.] *After l. 15, MS prints*: MIL-   *MS*.
FORD. Is your father gone to bed?

MILFORD.

I believe I had better avoid your father for the present.

HARRY.

I think you had. Dad considers you as my tempter, the cause of my ruin.

MILFORD.

And I being in his debt, he conceives he may treat me without ceremony.   20

HARRY.

Nay, damn it, Jack, do him justice! It is not the money you had of him, but the ill advice he imputes to you that galls him.

MILFORD.

I hear he threatens to arrest me.

HARRY.

Yes! He has threatened to strike my name out of the firm,   25 and disinherit me, a thousand times!

MILFORD.

Oh, but he has been very serious in menacing me.

HARRY.

And me too.

MILFORD.

You'll be at the tennis court tomorrow?

HARRY.

No.   30

MILFORD.

What, not to see the grand match?

HARRY.

No.

MILFORD.

Oh yes, you will.

HARRY.

No. I am determined.

MILFORD.

Yes, overnight; you'll waver in the morning.   35

HARRY.

No. It is high time, Jack, to grow prudent.

MILFORD.

Ha, ha, ha! My plan is formed; I'll soon be out of debt.

HARRY.

How will you get the money?

MILFORD.

By calculation.

HARRY.

Ha, ha, ha!   40

MILFORD.

I am resolved on it. What! Can't a man of invention and
genius outwit a blackleg?

HARRY.

Yes, if he will be as great a scoundrel.

MILFORD.

That's not necessary. A keen eye, a contriving head, a lucky
moment and a little algebra will rout the whole host. How   45
many men of rank and honor, having lost their fortunes,
have doubly recovered them!

HARRY.

And very honorably!

MILFORD.

Who doubts it?

HARRY.

Ha, ha, ha! Nobody! Nobody!   50

MILFORD.

But pray, Harry, what is it you find so attractive in my late
father's amorous relict?

HARRY.

Ha, ha, ha! What, the widow Warren?

MILFORD.

She seems to think and even reports you are to marry!

HARRY.

Marry? Her? A coquette of forty, who ridiculously apes all   55
the airs of a girl! Fantastic, selfish, and a fool! And marry?
Disgusting idea! Thou wert philosophizing as we drove on
the condition of a post horse—?

MILFORD.

Well?

41–45. What! ... host] *cancelled*
MS; om. Inch., Ox.

HARRY.

I would rather be a post horse, nay, the rascal that drives a   60
post horse, than the base thing thou hast imagined!

MILFORD.

Then why are you so often there?

HARRY.

Because I can't keep away.

MILFORD.

What, it is her daughter, Sophia?

HARRY.

Lovely, bewitching innocent!   65

MILFORD.

The poor young thing is fond of you?

HARRY.

I should be half mad if I thought she was not, yet am obliged
to half hope she is not!

MILFORD.

Why?

HARRY.

What a question! Am I not a profligate, and in all prob-   70
ability ruined? Not even my father can overlook this
last affair! No! Heigho!

MILFORD.

The loss of my father's will, and the mystery made of its contents by those who witnessed it, are strange circumstances!

HARRY.

In which the widow triumphs. And you being a bastard, and   75
left by law to starve, she willingly pays obedience to laws so
wise.

MILFORD.

She refuses even to pay my debts.

HARRY.

And the worthy alderman, your father, being overtaken by
death in the south of France, carefully makes a will, and   80
then as carefully hides it where it is not to be found; or
commits it to the custody of some mercenary knave, who has

60. rascal] brute *Q12, Ox.*

72. *Heigho*] Here and following this exclamation usually indicates a sigh.

-17-

made his market of it to the widow— So! Here comes the supposed executor of this supposed will.

Enter Mr. Sulky.

My dear Mr. Sulky, how do you do?   85

SULKY.

Very ill.

HARRY.

Indeed? I am very sorry! What's your disorder?

SULKY.

You.

HARRY.

Ha, ha, ha!

SULKY.

Ruin, bankruptcy, infamy!   90

HARRY.

The old story!

SULKY.

To a new tune.

HARRY.

Ha, ha, ha!

SULKY.

You are—

HARRY.

What, my good cynic?   95

SULKY.

A fashionable gentleman.

HARRY.

I know it.

SULKY.

And fashionably ruined.

HARRY.

No—I have a father.

SULKY.

Who is ruined likewise.   100

HARRY.

Ha, ha, ha! Is the Bank of England ruined?

SULKY.

I say ruined. Nothing less than a miracle can save the house.
The purse of Fortunatus could not supply you.

HARRY.

No; it held nothing but guineas. Notes, bills, paper for me!

SULKY.

Such effrontery is insufferable. For these five years, sir, you 105
have been driving to ruin more furiously than—

HARRY.

An ambassador's coach on a birthnight. I saw you were
stammering for a simile.

SULKY.

Sir!

HARRY.

Youth mounts the box, seizes the reins, and jehus headlong 110
on in the dark; Passion and Prodigality blaze in the front,
bewilder the coachman, and dazzle and blind the pas-
sengers; Wisdom, Prudence, and Virtue are overset and
maimed or murdered; and at last Repentance, like the
footman's flambeau lagging behind, lights us to dangers 115
when they are past all remedy.

SULKY.

Your name is struck off the firm. I was the advisor.

HARRY.

You were very kind, Mr. Sulky.

SULKY.

Your father is at last determined.

HARRY.

Ha, ha, ha! Do you think so?   120

SULKY.

You'll find so! (*To* Milford.) And what brought you
here, sir?

---

103. *purse of Fortunatus*] an inexhaustible purse. Fortunatus, the beggar
hero of a popular European tale, received from Fortune a purse which
contained an ever replenished supply of coins. The earliest known published
version of the tale appeared in 1509, and an English dramatization by
Thomas Dekker was printed in 1600.

107. *birthnight*] the court festival held on the evening of a royal birthday
(*OED*).

110. *jehus*] drives furiously; II Kings 9:20.

MILFORD.

A chaise and four.

SULKY.

It might have carried you to a safer place. When do you
mean to pay your debts? 125

MILFORD.

When my father's executor prevails on the widow Warren
to do me justice.

SULKY.

And which way am I to prevail?

MILFORD.

And which way am I to pay my debts?

SULKY.

You might have more modesty than insolentl, to come and 130
brave one of your principal creditors, after having ruined
his son by your evil counsel.

HARRY.

Ha, ha, ha! Don't believe a word on't, my good grumbler; I
ruined myself, I wanted no counselor.

MILFORD.

My father died immensely rich; and, though I am what the 135
law calls illegitimate, I ought not to starve.

SULKY.

You have had five thousand pounds, and are five more in
debt.

MILFORD.

Yes, thanks to those who trust boys with thousands.

SULKY.

You would do the same now you think yourself a man. 140

MILFORD (*firmly*).

Indeed I would not.

SULKY.

Had you been watching the widow at home, instead of
galloping after a knot of gamblers and pickpockets, you
might perhaps have done yourself more service.

MILFORD.

Which way, sir? 145

140. now you think] now, that you
think *Q 12, Inch., Ox.*

SULKY.

The will of your late father is found.

MILFORD.

Found?

SULKY.

I have received a letter, from which I learn it was at last
discovered, carefully locked up in a private drawer; and
that it is now a full month since a gentleman of Montpelier, 150
coming to England, was entrusted with it. But no such
gentleman has yet appeared.

MILFORD.

If it should have got into the hands of the widow—!

SULKY.

Which I suspect it has! —You are a couple of pretty gentlemen! But beware! Misfortune is at your heels! Mr. Dornton 155
vows vengeance on you both, and justly. He is not gone to
bed; and if you have confidence enough to look him in the
face, I would have you stay where you are.

MILFORD.

I neither wish to insult nor be insulted.   *Exit.*

SULKY.

Do you know, sir, your father turned the poor fellow into 160
the street, who compassionately opened the door for you?

HARRY.

Yes; and my father knows I as compassionately opened the
door for the poor fellow in return.

SULKY.

Very well, sir! Your fame is increasing daily.

HARRY.

I am glad to hear it.   165

SULKY.

Humph! Then perhaps you have paragraphed yourself?

HARRY.

Paragraphed? What? Where?

SULKY.

In the *St. James's Evening.*

HARRY.

Me?

SULKY.

Stating the exact amount.   170

HARRY.

Of my loss?

SULKY.

Yours. You march through every avenue to fame, dirty or
clean.

HARRY.

Well said! Be witty when you can; sarcastic you must be,
in spite of your teeth. But I like you the better. You are 175
honest. You are my cruet of cayenne, and a sprinkling of
you is excellent.

SULKY.

Well, sir, when you know the state of your own affairs, and
to what you have reduced the house, you will perhaps be
less ready to grin.   180

HARRY.

Reduced the house! Ha, ha, ha!

Enter Mr. Dornton, *with the newspaper in his hand.*

DORNTON.

So, sir!

HARRY (*bowing*).

I am happy to see you, sir.

DORNTON.

You are there, after having broken into my house at midnight! And you are here [*pointing to the paper*], after having 185
ruined me and my house by your unprincipled prodigality!
Are you not a scoundrel?

HARRY.

No, sir; I am only a fool.

SULKY.

Good night to you, gentlemen.

DORNTON.

Stay where you are, Mr. Sulky. I beg you to stay where you 190
are, and be a witness to my solemn renunciation of him
and his vices!

SULKY.

I have witnessed it a thousand times.

174–175. *sarcastic . . . teeth*] Sulky has poor or missing teeth.

DORNTON.

But this is the last. Are you not a scoundrel, I say?

HARRY.

I am your son.   195

DORNTON (*calling*).

Mr. Smith! Bring in those deeds.

Enter Mr. Smith.

You will not deny you are an incorrigible squanderer?

HARRY.

I will deny nothing.

DORNTON.

A nuisance, a wart, a blot, a stain upon the face of nature!

HARRY.

A stain that will wash out, sir.   200

DORNTON.

A redundancy, a negation; a besotted sophisticated incum-
brance; a jumble of fatuity; your head, your heart, your
words, your actions, all a jargon; incoherent and unintelli-
gible to yourself, absurd and offensive to others!

SULKY.

The whirlwind is rising.   205

HARRY.

I am whatever you please, sir.

DORNTON.

Bills never examined, everything bought on credit, the price
of nothing asked! Conscious you were weak enough to wish
for baubles you did not want, and pant for pleasures you
could not enjoy, you had not the effrontery to assume the   210
circumspect caution of common sense! And to your other
destructive follies, you must add the detestable vice of
gaming!

HARRY.

These things, sir, are much easier done than defended.

DORNTON.

But here—[*to* Mr. Smith]—give me that parchment! The   215
partners have all been summoned. Look, sir! Your name
has been formally erased!

205.] *Om. Ox.*

−23−

HARRY.

　　The partners are very kind.

DORNTON.

　　The suspicions already incurred by the known profligacy of
　　a principal in the firm, the immense sums you have drawn,　220
　　this paragraph, the run on the house it will occasion, the
　　consternation of the whole city—

HARRY (*half aside*).

　　All very terrible, and some of it very true.

DORNTON (*passionately*).

　　Give me the will, Mr. Smith! Give me the will! Fond and
　　foolish as I have been, read, and you will find I am at last　225
　　restored to my senses! If I should happily outlive the storm
　　you have raised, it shall not be to support a prodigal, or to
　　reward a gambler! You are disinherited! Read!

HARRY.

　　Your word is as good as the Bank, sir.

DORNTON.

　　I'll no longer act the doting father, fascinated by your arts!　230

HARRY.

　　I never had any art, sir, except the one you taught me.

DORNTON.

　　I taught you! What? Scoundrel! What?

HARRY.

　　That of loving you, sir.

DORNTON.

　　Loving me!

HARRY.

　　Most sincerely!　　　　　　　　　　　　　　　　　235

DORNTON (*forgetting his passion*).

　　Why, can you say, Harry— Rascal! I mean, that you love
　　me?

HARRY.

　　I should be a rascal indeed if I did not, sir.

DORNTON (*struggling with his feelings*).

　　Harry! Harry! No! Confound me if I do! Sir, you are a
　　vile—!　　　　　　　　　　　　　　　　　　　240

224—226. Give . . . senses] *om. Ox.*

HARRY.

    I know I am.

DORNTON.

    And I'll never speak to you more.   *Going*.

HARRY.

    Bid me good night, sir. Mr. Sulky here will bid me good
night, and you are my father! —Good night, Mr. Sulky.

SULKY.

    Good night.   *Exit.*   245

HARRY.

    Come, sir—

DORNTON (*struggling with passion*).

    I won't! If I do—!

HARRY.

    Reproach me with my follies, strike out my name, disinherit
me, I deserve it all and more—but say good night, Harry!

DORNTON.

    I won't! I won't! I won't!   250

HARRY.

    Poverty is a trifle; we can whistle it off. But enmity!

DORNTON.

    I will not!

HARRY.

    Sleep in enmity? And who can say how soundly? Come!
Good night.

DORNTON.

    I won't! I won't!   *Runs off.*   255

HARRY.

    Say you so? Why, then, my noble-hearted dad, I am indeed
a scoundrel!

Re-enter Mr. Dornton.

DORNTON.

    Good night!   *Exit.*

HARRY.

    Good night! And Heaven eternally bless you, sir! Heigho!
That's something.   *Sings.*   260

259–266. And . . . Heigho] *om. Ox.*   260–266. That's . . . Heigho] *om.
Inch.*

> *Time, would you let him wisely pass,*
> *Is lively, brisk and jolly.*

All is not quite as it should be; but—   *Sings.*

> *Dip but his wings in the sparkling glass,*
> *And he'll drown dull melancholy.*   265

Heigho!   *Exit.*

ACT II

The house of the Widow Warren.
                    Jenny *and* Mrs. Ledger.

JENNY.

   I tell you, good woman, I can do nothing for you.

MRS. LEDGER.

   Only let me see Mrs. Warren.

JENNY.

   And get myself snubbed. Not I indeed.

                    Enter Sophia, *skipping.*

SOPHIA.

   La, Jenny! Yonder's my mamma, with a whole congregation
   of manteaumakers, mercers, haberdashers, lacemen, feather-   5
   men, and—and all the world, consulting about second
   mourning!

JENNY.

   I know it.

SOPHIA.

   It will be six months tomorrow since the death of my father-
   in-law; and she has been busy giving orders for this fortnight   10
   that everything might be brought home and tried on today.
   I do believe she'll sleep in her new clothes!

JENNY.

   How you run on, miss!

SOPHIA.

   What would my dear grandma say, if she saw her? Why,
   she is even fonder of finery than I am!   15

JENNY.

   Sure, miss, you are not fond of finery?

SOPHIA.

   Oh, but I am. I wonder why she won't let me wear high-
   heeled shoes! I am sure I am old enough! I shall be eighteen
   next Christmas Day at midnight, which is only nine months
   and two days! And since she likes to wear slips, and sashes,   20
   and ringlets and—nonsense, like a girl, why should not I

9–10. *father-in-law*] stepfather.

have high heels, and gowns, and sestinis, and hoops, and
trains, and sweeps [*mimicking*] and—like a woman?

JENNY.

It's very true what your mamma tells you, miss; you have
been spoiled by your old fond grandmother in Gloucester-   25
shire.

SOPHIA.

Nay, Jenny, I won't hear you call my dear grandma names!
Though everybody told the loving old soul she would spoil me.

JENNY.

And now your mamma has sent for you up to town to finish
your edication.   30

SOPHIA.

Yes. She began it the very first day. There was the staymaker
sent for, to screw up my shapes; the shoemaker, to cripple
my feet; the hairdresser, to burn my hair; the jeweller, to
bore my ears; and the dentist, to file my teeth.

JENNY.

Ah! You came here such a hoyden! (*To* Mrs. Ledger.)   35
What, an't you gone yet, mistress?

SOPHIA.

La, Jenny, how can you be so cross to people? What is the
matter with this good woman?

JENNY.

Oh, nothing but poverty.

SOPHIA (*rummaging her pocket*).

Is that all? Here, give her this half crown, and make her   40
rich.

JENNY.

Rich indeed!

SOPHIA.

What, is not it enough? La, I am sorry I spent all my money
yesterday! I laid it out in sweetmeats, cakes, a canary bird,
and a poll parrot. But I hope you are not very, very poor?   45

MRS. LEDGER.

My husband served the late alderman five-and-twenty years.
His master promised to provide for him; but his pitiless

22–23. sestinis, and hoops, and   *Inch.*; satins, and trains *Ox.*
trains] festinis, and hoops, and trains   30. edication] iddication *Q12, Ox.*

widow can see him thrown with a broken heart upon the parish.

SOPHIA.

> Oh, dear! Stop! Stop a bit! (*Running off.*) Be sure you 50
> don't go! *Exit.*

Enter Mr. Sulky.

SULKY.

> Where's your mistress, girl?

JENNY.

> My name is Jane Cocket, sir.

SULKY.

> Where's your mistress?

JENNY.

> Busy, sir. 55

SULKY.

> Tell her to come down. Don't stare, girl, but go and tell your mistress I want her.

JENNY (*aside*).

> Humph! Mr. Black and gruff! *Exit.*

Re-enter Sophia, *with great glee.*

SOPHIA.

> I've got it! Here! Take this, good woman; go home and be happy! Take it, I tell you! *Offering a purse.* 60

SULKY.

> Who is this? Mrs. Ledger! How does your worthy husband?

MRS. LEDGER.

> Alack, sir, ill enough: likely to starve in his latter days.

SULKY.

> How! Starve?

MRS. LEDGER.

> The widow refuses to do anything for him.

SULKY.

> Humph! 65

MRS. LEDGER.

> Service, age, and honesty are poor pleas, with affluence, ease, and Mrs. Warren.

SULKY.

> Humph!

MRS. LEDGER.

> You, sir, I understand, are the late alderman's executor?

SULKY.

> I can't tell.   70

MRS. LEDGER.

> Perhaps you may be able to serve my husband?

SULKY.

> I don't know. However, give my respects to him. He shan't
> starve; tell him that.

SOPHIA.

> Nay, but take this in the meantime.

SULKY.

> Ay; take it, take it.   *Exit* Mrs. Ledger *much affected.*   75
> And who are you, Miss Charity?

SOPHIA.

> Me, sir? Oh! I—I am my grandma's granddaughter.

SULKY.

> Humph!

SOPHIA.

> Sophia Freelove.

SULKY.

> Oh! The widow's daughter by her first husband?   80

SOPHIA.

> Yes, sir.

Re-enter Jenny.

SULKY.

> Where's your mistress?

JENNY.

> Coming, sir. —So! You have stolen your mamma's purse,
> miss?

SOPHIA.

> La, don't say so; I only ran away with it! She was bargaining   85
> for some smuggled lace with one of your acquaintance, and
> I thought I could dispose of her money to better advantage.

JENNY.

> Without her consent?

85. ran] run *Q12, Inch.*

SOPHIA.

Yes, to be sure! I knew I should never dispose of it in that
manner with her consent.   90

JENNY.

Well! Here comes your mamma.   *Exit.*

Enter the Widow Warren, *in a fantastic girlish morning dress, surrounded
by* Milliners, Manteaumakers, Furriers, Hatters, *&c., with their*
Attendants *with bandboxes, all talking as they come on.*

WIDOW.

So you'll be sure not to forget my chapeau à la Prusse, Mr.
Mincing?

HATTER.

Certainly not, madam.

WIDOW.

And you'll make a delicate choice of the feathers?   95

HATTER.

The selection shall be elegant, madam.

WIDOW.

Yes—I know, Mr. Mincing, you're a charming man! —And
you will let me have my pierrot à la Coblentz by nine in the
morning, Mrs. Tiffany?

MANTEAUMAKER.

To a minute, maim.   100

SULKY.

Madam, when you have a moment's leisure—

WIDOW.

Be quiet, you fright; don't interrupt me! —And my caraco à
la hussar, and my bavaroises à la duchesse. And put four
rows of pearl in my turban.

MILLINER.

Ver well, me ladyship.   105

91.] *om. MS.*   102–103. And . . . duchesse] And my
                                  fichu menteur, Mrs. La Blonde *MS.*

---

98. *pierrot*] a woman's low-necked blouse with sleeves.
102. *caraco*] a gown with a long, tight-fitting bodice, finished with a
peplum ruffle, adapted from a man's short coat with tails.
103. *bavaroise*] feminine version of a man's frock coat.

WIDOW.

> And you'll all come together, exactly at nine?

OMNES.

> We'll all be here!   *Going.*

WIDOW.

> And don't forget the white ermine tippets, and the black fox muffs, and the Kamschatka furs that you mentioned, Mr. Weazel!   110

FURRIER.

> I'll bring a fine assortment, madam.

WIDOW.

> And, and, and—no; no—you may all go—I can think of nothing else—I shall remember more tomorrow.

HATTER AND FURRIER.

> Thank you, madam!

MANTEAUMAKER AND GIRLS.

> Very much obliged to you, maim!   *All together.*   115

MILLINER.

> Dee ver good bon jour to me ladyship.   *Exeunt.*

WIDOW.

> What was it you were saying, Mr. Sulky? —Pray, child, what have you done with my purse?

SOPHIA.

> Given it away, ma.

WIDOW.

> Given it away, minikin?   120

SOPHIA.

> Yes, ma.

WIDOW.

> Given my purse away! To whom? For what purpose?

SOPHIA.

> La, ma, only—only to keep a poor woman from starving!

WIDOW.

> I protest, child, your grandmother has totally ruined you!

SULKY.

> Not quite, madam: she has left the finishing to you.   125

WIDOW.

> What were you saying, Mr. Sulky?

SULKY.

> You won't give me leave to say anything, madam.

WIDOW.

You know you are a shocking troublesome man, Mr. Sulky!
I have a thousand things to remember, and can't bear
teasing! It fatigues my spirits! So pray relate this very 130
urgent business of yours in a single word. What would you
have?

SULKY.

Justice.

WIDOW.

Lord, what do you mean? Do you think I am in the com-
mission?   135

SULKY.

Yes, of follies innumerable!

WIDOW.

You are a sad savage, Mr. Sulky! And who is it you want
justice for?

SULKY.

Your late husband's son, John Milford.

WIDOW.

Now pray don't talk to me! You are a very intrusive person! 140
You quite derange my ideas! I can think of nothing soft or
satisfactory while you are present!

SULKY.

Will you hear me, madam?

WIDOW.

I can't! I positively can't! It is an odious subject!

SOPHIA.

Nah, ma, how can you be so cross to my brother Milford? 145

WIDOW.

Your brother, child? Country education! How often,
minikin, have I told you he is no brother of yours!

SOPHIA.

La, ma, he was your husband's son!

WIDOW.

Yes, his—faugh! Odious word! Your brother?

SOPHIA.

Yes, that he is! For he is in distress.   150

134. mean? Do] mean—Odious   149. Yes, his—] Yes, his ba— *Ox.*
word. Do *MS.*

SULKY.

Humph!

WIDOW.

And would you now, you who pretend to be a very prudent
—ridiculous kind of a person, wish to see me squander the
wealth of my poor dear dead good man on Mr. Milford, and
his profligate companions?   155

SULKY.

Not I indeed, madam, though the profligate to whom you
make love should happen to be one of them!

WIDOW.

Ha, ha, ha! Oh, the monster! I make love! You have no eyes,
Mr. Sulky! (*Walking and exhibiting herself.*) You are
really blind! But I know whom you mean.   160

SULKY.

I mean young Dornton, madam.

WIDOW.

To be sure you do! Whom could you mean? Elegant youth!
Rapturous thoughts!

SOPHIA.

I am sure, sir, young Mr. Dornton is no profligate!

SULKY (*significantly*).

You are sure?   165

SOPHIA.

Yes, that I am!

SULKY.

Humph.

SOPHIA.

And it's very scandalous, very scandalous indeed, to say he
is my ma's lover!

SULKY.

Humph.   170

SOPHIA.

Because he is a fine genteel young gentleman; and you know
ma is—

WIDOW.

Pray, minikin, be less flippant with your tongue.

152. you who] Mr. Sulky, who *MS*.   160. whom] who *MS*.

SOPHIA.

Why, la, ma, you yourself know you are too—!

WIDOW.

Go up to your chamber, child!   175

SOPHIA.

I am sure, ma, I say it is very scandalous to call the handsome Mr. Dornton your lover!   *Exit skipping.*

SULKY.

Do you blush?

WIDOW.

Blush indeed? Blush? Ha, ha, ha! You are a very unaccountable creature, Mr. Sulky! Blush at the babbling of a child? 180

SULKY.

Who is your rival?

WIDOW.

Ha, ha, ha, ha, ha! My rival? The poor minikin! My
rival? —But I have a message for you! Now do compose
your features to softness and complacency! Look pleasant
if you can! Smile for once in your life!   185

SULKY.

Don't make love to me! I'll have nothing to say to you!

WIDOW.

Ha, ha, ha! Love?

SULKY.

Yes, you make love to Dornton! Nay, you make love to the
booby Goldfinch! Even I am not secure in your company!

WIDOW.

Ha, ha, ha! You are a shocking being, Mr. Sulky! But if you 190
should happen to see Mr. Dornton, do astonish your
acquaintance: do a good-natured thing, and tell him I am
at home all day. Love to you? Ha, ha, ha! Oh, you figure!
You caricatura of tenderness! You insupportable thing!   *Exit.*

SULKY (*sighs*).

Ah! All labor in vain!   195

Enter Jenny.

Stand out of the way, girl!   *Exit.*

JENNY (*looking after the* Widow).

There she goes! That's lucky! This way, sir!

Enter Harry Dornton, *followed by his own* Servant *with bills in his hand.*

My mistress is gone up to her toilette, sir; but I can send you
somebody you may like better!   *Exit.*

HARRY.

Obliging Abigail! (*Looking over his papers.*) 'Sdeath! 200
What, all these tradesmen's bills?

SERVANT.

All, sir. Mr. Smith sent me after you with them.

HARRY.

When were they brought?

SERVANT.

Some last night, but most this morning.

HARRY.

Ill news travels fast, and honesty is devilish industrious. Go 205
round to them all, return their bills, and bid them come
themselves today. Has Mr. Williams the hosier sent in his
bill?

SERVANT.

No, sir.

HARRY.

I thought as much. Tell him to come with the rest, and on 210
his life not fail.

SERVANT.

Very well, sir.   *Exit.*

Enter Sophia *joyously.*

SOPHIA.

Oh, Mr. Dornton, I am glad to see you! Do you know, I've
got the song by heart that you was so good as to teach me!

HARRY.

And do you know, my charming Sophia, you are the most 215
delightful, beautiful, bewitching scholar that ever took
lesson!

SOPHIA.

La, Mr. Dornton, I'm sure I'm very stupid!

HARRY.

That you are all intelligence, all grace, all wit!

---

200. *Abigail*] lady's maid, from the waiting gentlewoman in Beaumont
and Fletcher's *The Scornful Lady*, 1613–1616.

SOPHIA.

To be sure my ma caught me singing it, and she was pettish; 220
because you know it's all about love, and ends with a happy
marriage.

HARRY.

But why pettish?

SOPHIA.

La, I can't tell. I suppose she wants to have all the marriage
in the world to herself! It's her whole talk! I do believe 225
she'd be married every morning that she rises, if anybody
would have her!

HARRY.

Think not of her, my sweet Sophia, but tell me—

SOPHIA.

What?

HARRY.

I dare not ask.   230

SOPHIA.

Why?

HARRY.

Lest I should offend you.

SOPHIA.

Nay, now, Mr. Dornton, that is not right of you! I am never
offended with anybody, and I am sure I should not be
offended with you! My grandma always said I was the 235
best-tempered girl in the world. What is it?

HARRY (*taking her hand*).

Were you—? Did you ever know what it is to love?

SOPHIA.

La, now, how could you ask one such a question? You know
very well one must not tell! Besides, you know too one must
not be in love!   240

HARRY.

Why not?

SOPHIA.

Because—because I'm but a girl. My grandma has told me a
hundred times, it's a sin for anybody to be in love before
they be a woman grown, full one-and-twenty; and I am not
eighteen!   245

HARRY.

Love they say cannot be resisted.

SOPHIA.

Ah, but I have been taught better! It may be resisted.
Nobody need be in love unless they like; and so I won't be
in love, for I won't wilfully do amiss. (*With great positive-
ness.*)   No! I won't love any person, though I should love 250
him ever dearly!

HARRY (*aside*).

Angelic innocence!   (*Aloud.*)   Right, lovely Sophia, guard
your heart against seducers.

SOPHIA.

Do you know, it is full five weeks since Valentine's Day;
and, because I'm not one-and-twenty, nobody sent me a 255
valentine!

HARRY.

And did you expect one?

SOPHIA.

Nah! I can't say but I did think—! In Gloucestershire, if
any young man happen to have a liking for a young woman,
she is sure to hear of it on Valentine's Day. But perhaps 260
Valentine's Day does not fall so soon here as it does in the
country?

HARRY.

Why, it is possible you may yet receive a valentine.

SOPHIA.

Nay, now, but don't you go to think that I am asking for
one; for that would be very wrong of me, and I know better. 265
My grandma told me I must never mention nor think of such
things till I am a woman, full one-and-twenty grown; and
that if I were to find such a thing at my window, or under
my pillow, or concealed in a plumcake—

HARRY.

A plumcake?   270

SOPHIA.

Yes, I assure you I have heard of a valentine sent baked in a

251. ever dearly] ever so dearly   259. happen] happens *MS*, *Q12*,
MS, *Q4–6*, *Q9–12*, *Inch.*, *Ox.*   *Inch.*, *Ox.*

plumcake. —And so if I had one that I must show it to her.
But you know she is in Gloucestershire; and I am sure I
would not show it to ma, for though she is all out and above
forty, she would be as jealous as the vengeance! And indeed I   275
would not receive such a thing for the world, no, not from
the finest man on earth, if I did not think him to be a true
and faithful, true, true lover!

HARRY.

But how must he prove his faith and truth?

SOPHIA.

Why, first he must love me very dearly! With all his heart   280
and soul! And then he must be willing to wait till I am one-
and-twenty.

HARRY.

And would not you love in return?

SOPHIA.

N—yes, when I come to be one-and-twenty.

HARRY.

Not sooner?   285

SOPHIA.

Oh, no! I must not!

HARRY.

Surely you might if you pleased?

SOPHIA.

Oh, but you must not persuade me to that! If you do I shall
think you are a bad man, such as my grandma warned me
of!   290

HARRY.

And do you think me so?

SOPHIA.

Do I? No! I would not think you so for a thousand thousand
golden guineas!

HARRY (aside).

Fascinating purity! What am I about? To deceive or trifle
with such unsuspecting affection would indeed be villainy!   295

GOLDFINCH (without, at a distance).

Is she above? Must see her!

272–275. if I . . . indeed] om. Inch.;   274. and above] om. MS.
if I . . . vengeance om. Ox.

SOPHIA.

La, I hear that great, ridiculous, horse-jockey oaf Goldfinch
coming up! (*Sighs.*)   Good-bye, Mr. Dornton!

HARRY.

Heaven bless you, Sophia! Sweet Sophia, Heaven bless you,
my lovely angel! Heigho!   300

SOPHIA.

Heigho!   *Exit.*

GOLDFINCH (*without*).

Is she here?

SERVANT (*without*).

I don't know, sir.

Enter Goldfinch *in a high-collared coat, several under-waistcoats, buckskin
breeches covering his calves, short boots, long spurs, high-crowned hat, hair in
the extreme, &c.*

GOLDFINCH.

Hah! My tight one!

HARRY (*surveying him*).

Well, Charles!   305

GOLDFINCH.

How you stare! An't I the go? That's your sort!

HARRY.

Ha, ha, ha!

GOLDFINCH.

Where's the widow?

HARRY.

Gone up to dress, and will not be down these two hours.

GOLDFINCH.

A hundred to eighty I'd sup up a string of twenty horses in 310
less time than she takes to dress her fetlocks, plait her mane,
trim her ears, and buckle on her body clothes!

HARRY.

You improve daily, Charles!

GOLDFINCH.

To be sure! That's your sort!   (*Turning round to show himself.*)   An't I a *genus*?   315

297. oaf Goldfinch] of Goldfinch
Q12; Goldfinch *Ox.*

304. *tight one*] competent, smart.
306. *the go*] the rage, height of fashion.
310. *sup up . . . horses*] give the last feeding of the day to.

HARRY.

Quite an original! You may challenge the whole fraternity
of the whip to match you!

GOLDFINCH.

Match me! Newmarket can't match me!   (*Showing himself.*)
That's your sort!

HARRY.

Oh, no! Ha, ha, ha! You are harder to match than one of   320
your own pied ponies. —A very different being from either
your father or grandfather!

GOLDFINCH.

Father or grandfather! Shakebags both.

HARRY.

How!

GOLDFINCH.

Father a sugarbaker, grandfather a slopseller. I'm a gentle-   325
man—that's your sort!

HARRY.

Ha, ha, ha! And your father was only a man of worth.

GOLDFINCH (*with great contempt*).

Kept a gig! Knew nothing of life! Never drove four!

HARRY.

No, but he was a useful member of society.

GOLDFINCH.

A usef—! What's that?   330

HARRY.

Ha, ha, ha! A pertinent question.

GOLDFINCH.

A gentleman like me a useful member of society! Bet the
long odds nobody ever heard of such a thing!

HARRY.

You have not acquired your character in the world for
nothing, Charles.   335

GOLDFINCH.

World! What does the world say?

HARRY.

Strange things. It says you have got into the hands of

---

323. *Shakebags*] men of no spirit.
328. *gig*] light two-wheeled carriage drawn by only one horse.

jockeys, Jews, and swindlers; and that, though old Goldfinch was in his day one of the richest men on 'Change, his
son will shortly become poorer than the poorest blackleg at 340
Newmarket.

GOLDFINCH.

Damn the world!

HARRY.

With all my heart, damn the world, for it says little better of
me.

GOLDFINCH.

Bet you seven to five the Eclipse colts against the Highflyers, 345
the second spring meeting.

HARRY.

No. I have done with Highflyer and Eclipse too. —So you
are in pursuit of the widow?

GOLDFINCH.

Full cry! Must have her!

HARRY.

Ha, ha, ha! Heigho! You must?   350

GOLDFINCH.

All up with me else! If I don't marry the widow I must
smash! I've secured the knowing one.

HARRY.

Whom do you mean? The maid?

GOLDFINCH.

Promised her a hundred on the wedding day.

Enter Jenny.

JENNY.

My mistress can't see you at present, gentlemen.   355

GOLDFINCH.

Can't see me? (*Vexed.*)   Take Harriet an airing in the
phaeton!

353. Whom] Who *MS*.

---

346. *spring meeting*] one of seven annual race meetings at Newmarket.

347. *Highflyer*] 1774–1793, famous race horse, whose purchase laid the
foundation of Richard Tattersall's fortune.

347. *Eclipse*] 1764–1789, one of the greatest of all thoroughbred race
horses, never defeated.

HARRY.

What, is Harriet your favorite?

GOLDFINCH.

To be sure! I keep her.

HARRY.

You do?   360

GOLDFINCH.

Fine creature!

HARRY.

Well bred?

GOLDFINCH.

Just to my taste! Like myself, free and easy. That's your
sort!

HARRY.

A fine woman?   365

GOLDFINCH.

Prodigious! Sister to the Irish Giant! Six feet in her stockings! That's your sort! Sleek coat, flowing mane, broad
chest, all bone! Dashing figure in a phaeton! Sky-blue habit,
scarlet sash, green hat, yellow ribbands, white feathers, gold
band and tassel! That's your sort!   370

HARRY.

Ha, ha, ha! Heigho! Why, you are a high fellow, Charles!

GOLDFINCH.

To be sure! Know the odds! Hold four in hand! Turn a
corner in style! Reins in form—elbows square—wrist pliant
—hayait! Drive the Coventry stage twice a week all
summer—pay for an inside place—mount the box—tip the   375
coachy a crown—beat the mail—come in full speed! Rattle
down the gateway! Take care of your heads! Never killed
but one woman and a child in all my life—that's your sort!

Going.

JENNY (*aside to* Goldfinch).

Take him with you.   *Exit.*

---

366. *Irish Giant*] probably Charles Byrne (sometimes confused with
Patrick O'Brien), 1761–1783, reputed to be 8 feet, 4 inches tall, whose
skeleton is preserved in the museum of the Royal College of Surgeons,
London.

GOLDFINCH.

Want a hedge? Take guineas to pounds Precipitate against 380
Dragon?

HARRY.

No.

GOLDFINCH (*aside*).

Wish I could have him a few! (*Drawing his hand clenched
from his pocket.*)   Odd or even for fifty?

HARRY.

Ha, ha, ha! Odd enough! 385

GOLDFINCH.

Will you cut a card, hide in the hat, chuck in the glass, draw
cuts, heads or tails, gallop the maggot, swim the hedgehog,
anything?

HARRY.

Nothing.

GOLDFINCH.

I'm up to all. That's your sort!   (*Aside.*)   Get him with me 390
and pigeon him. —Come and see my greys. Been to Tattersall's and bought a set of six. Smokers! Beat all England for
figure, bone, and beauty! Hayait, charmers! That's your
sort! Bid for two pair of mouse ponies for Harriet.

HARRY.

Ha, ha, ha! The Irish Giantess drawn by mouse ponies! 395

GOLDFINCH.

Come and see 'em.

HARRY (*sarcastically*).

No. I am weary of the company of stableboys.

GOLDFINCH.

Why so? Shan't play you any tricks. If they squirt water at
you, or make the colts kick you, tell me, and I'll horsewhip
'em. Arch dogs! Deal of wit! 400

380–381. Precipitate against Dra-
gon] Meteor against Sir Peter *MS.*

380–381. *Precipitate against Dragon*] In 1791 Dragon beat Precipitate at
the first spring meeting at Newmarket.

386–391. *Will . . . him*] contemporary gambling terms.

391. *Tattersall's*] a famous horse market, and the headquarters of credit
betting on English horse races, established in 1766 by Richard Tattersall.

394. *mouse ponies*] dun in color.

HARRY.

When they do I'll horsewhip them myself.

GOLDFINCH.

Yourself? 'Ware that! Wrong there!

HARRY.

I think I should be right.

GOLDFINCH.

Do you! What—been to school?

HARRY.

To school! Why, yes, I—   405

GOLDFINCH.

Mendoza! Oh! Good morrow!   *Exit.*

HARRY.

Ha, ha, ha! There goes one of my friends! Heigho!

Enter Milford *in haste, followed by* Goldfinch *returning.*

GOLDFINCH (*eagerly*).

What is it, Jack? Tell me!

MILFORD.

Come, Harry! We shall be too late! They are about to begin!
We may have what bets we please!   410

GOLDFINCH.

Where? What?

MILFORD.

The great match! The famous Frenchman and Will the
marker! A thousand guineas a side!

GOLDFINCH.

What, tennis?

MILFORD.

Yes. The Frenchman gives fifteen and a bisque.   415

GOLDFINCH.

To Will the marker?

MILFORD.

Yes.

415. fifteen and a bisque] a bisque
and half court *MS.*

404–406. *Been to ... Mendoza*] the boxing school of Daniel Mendoza
(1764–1836), famous pugilist, which marks a period in the history of prize
fighting (*DNB*).
415. *a bisque*] odds of one point.

GOLDFINCH.

    Will for a hundred!

MILFORD.

    Done!

GOLDFINCH.

    Done, done!   420

HARRY.

    I bar the bet; the odds are five to four already.

GOLDFINCH.

    What, for the mounseer?

HARRY.

    Yes.

GOLDFINCH.

    I'll take it, five hundred to four.

HARRY.

    Done!   425

GOLDFINCH.

    Done, done!

HARRY.

    No, I bar! I forgot—I have cut. I'll never bet another guinea.

MILFORD.

    You do for a hundred!

HARRY.

    Done!   430

MILFORD.

    Done, done! Ha, ha, ha!

HARRY.

    Pshaw!

GOLDFINCH.

    What a cake!

MILFORD.

    But you'll go?

HARRY.

    No.   435

MILFORD.

    Yes, you will. Come, come, the match is begun! Everybody is there! The Frenchman is the first player in the world!

---

427. *cut*] sworn off.
433. *cake*] fool.

HARRY.

It's a noble exercise!

MILFORD.

Ay! Cato himself delighted in it!

HARRY.

Yes, it was much practised by the Romans.   440

GOLDFINCH.

The Romans! Who are they?

HARRY.

Ha, ha, ha!

MILFORD.

Ha, ha, ha! Will you go or will you not, Harry?

HARRY.

I can't, Jack. My conscience won't let me.

MILFORD.

Pshaw! Zounds, if we don't make haste it will be all over! 445

HARRY (*in a hurry*).

Do you think it will?   (*Stops short.*)   No—I won't—I must
not.

MILFORD (*taking hold of his arm*).

Come along, I tell you!

HARRY.

No.

MILFORD.

They have begun.   450

GOLDFINCH.

Have they? I'm off!   *Exit.*

MILFORD (*still struggling, and* Harry *retreating*).

What folly! Come along!

HARRY.

No. I will not.

MILFORD (*leaving him and going*).

Well, well, if you're so positive—

HARRY (*calling*).

Stay, Jack; stay—I'll walk up the street with you, but I 455
won't go in.

MILFORD.

Double or quits the hundred that you won of me last night
you do!

HARRY.

I don't for a thousand!

MILFORD.

No, no, the hundred.   460

HARRY.

I tell you I won't. I won't go in with you.

MILFORD.

Done for the hundred!

HARRY.

Done, done!   *Exeunt.*

[II.ii]

*Scene changes to the parlor of the tennis court. Markers passing and repassing
with rackets and balls. Sheriff's Officer, two Followers, and one of the
Markers.*

Shout.

MARKER.

Hurrah!

OFFICER.

Pray, is Mr. Milford in the court?

MARKER.

I'll bet you gold to silver the Frenchman loses! Hurrah!   *Exit.*

Enter Mr. Smith *from the court.*

MR. SMITH.

He is not there.

OFFICER.

Are you sure?   5

MR. SMITH.

The crowd is very great, but I can neither see him nor any
of his companions.

OFFICER.

Then he will not come.

MR. SMITH.

I begin to hope so!

OFFICER (*examining the writ*).

"Middlesex to wit—one thousand pounds—Dornton against   10
John Milford."

MR. SMITH.

You must take none but substantial bail. (*Shout.*) What
a scene!

OFFICER.

He will not be here.

MR. SMITH.

Heaven send!   15

Enter Goldfinch *and a* Marker *running across.*

GOLDFINCH.

Is the match begun?

MARKER.

The first game is just over.

GOLDFINCH.

Who lost?

MARKER.

The Frenchman!

GOLDFINCH.

Hurrah!   20

MARKER.

Hurrah!

GOLDFINCH.

Damn the mounseers! That's your sort!   *Exit into the court.*

MR. SMITH.

That's one of his companions. I begin to tremble. Stand
aside! Here they both come!

OFFICER.

Which is he?   25

MR. SMITH.

The second.   *Shout.*

Enter Harry Dornton *and* Milford, *in haste.*

HARRY.

I hear them! I hear them! Come along!

MILFORD.

Ha, ha, ha! Harry! You would not go! You were determined!   *Shout.*

HARRY.

Zounds! Come along!   *Exit in haste.*   30

Milford *follows him laughing.*

OFFICER (*stopping him*).

    A word with you, sir, if you please.

MILFORD.

    With me? Who are you? What do you want?

OFFICER.

    You are my prisoner.

MILFORD.

    Prisoner! Damnation! Let me go!

OFFICER.

    I must do my duty, sir.   35

MILFORD (*pulling out his purse*).

    Here, here; this is your duty.

MR. SMITH (*advancing*).

    It must not be, sir.

MILFORD.

    Mr. Smith! —What, at the suit of Dornton?

MR. SMITH.

    Yes, sir. 'Tis your own fault, for leading his son to these places. He heard you were to bring him here.   40

MILFORD.

    Furies! (*To a* Marker *passing*.) Marker! Tell Harry Dornton to come to me instantly!

MARKER.

    Yes, sir.   *Exit*.

Shout.

MILFORD.

    Zounds! Let me but go and see the match—

MR. SMITH.

    You must not, sir.   45

MILFORD (*to another* Marker).

    Marker!

MARKER.

    Sir!

MILFORD.

    Who wins?

39–40. for . . . places] Why do you
lead his son to these places *Q12, Ox*.

MARKER.

The Frenchman has the best on't.

MILFORD.

Tell Harry Dornton I am here in trouble. Desire him to   50
come this moment.

MARKER.

Very well, sir.   *Shout.*

MILFORD (*to the* Officer).

I'll give you ten guineas for five minutes!

MR. SMITH.

Take him away, sir.

OFFICER.

You must come along, sir.   55

MILFORD (*to a* Marker *returning*).

Have you told him?

MARKER.

He can't come, sir.

MILFORD.

Very well, Harry! Very well!   (*To the second* Marker.)
Well, sir?

MARKER.

He would not leave the court for a thousand pounds.   60

OFFICER.

Come, come, sir!   (*To his two Attendants.*)   Bring him
along!

MILFORD.

Hands off, scoundrels!   (*Shout.*)   Fiends!   *Exeunt.*

[II.iii]

Scene changes to the house of Mr. Silky. A room of business, ledger, letter
files, inkstand, &c. Silky *discovered, and* Jacob *entering.*

SILKY.

Well, Jacob! Have you been?

JACOB.

Yes, sir.

SILKY.

Well, and what news? How is he? Very bad?

JACOB.

Dead, sir.

SILKY (*overjoyed*).

    Dead?   5

JACOB.

    As Deborah!

SILKY (*aside*).

    I'm a lucky man! (*Aloud.*) Are you sure he is dead,
Jacob?

JACOB.

    I saw him with my own eyes, sir.

SILKY.

    That's right, Jacob! I'm a lucky man! And what say the   10
people at the hotel? Do they know who he is?

JACOB.

    Oh, yes, sir! He was rich! A gentleman in his own country!

SILKY.

    And did you take care they should not know you?

JACOB.

    To be sure, sir! You had given me my lesson!

SILKY.

    Ay, ay, Jacob! That's right! You are a fine boy! Mind me,   15
and I'll make a man of you! And you think they had heard
nothing of his having called on me?

JACOB.

    Not a word!

SILKY (*aside*).

    It was a lucky mistake! (*Aloud.*) Well, Jacob! Keep
close! Don't say a word, and I'll give you—I'll give you a   20
crown!

JACOB.

    You promised me a guinea, sir!

SILKY.

    Did I, Jacob? Did I? Well, well! I'll give you a guinea!
But be close! Did you call at the widow Warren's?

JACOB.

    Yes, sir.   25

---

10. I'm] I am *Q4, Q6, Q9–12.*   12. rich! A gentleman] a rich
                                                         gentleman *MS.*

  6. *Deborah*] perhaps referring to Genesis 35:8.

SILKY.

And will she see me?

JACOB.

She desires you will be there in an hour.

SILKY.

Very well, Jacob. Keep close! Not a word about the foreign
gentleman, or his having been here a week ago, or his being
taken suddenly ill and dying! (*Aside.*) It is a lucky   30
stroke! Close, Jacob, my boy!

JACOB.

But give me the guinea, sir!

SILKY.

What, now, Jacob?

JACOB.

If you please, sir. You may forget—

SILKY.

Well, there, Jacob; there! You'll be a rich man, Jacob! A   35
cunning fellow! I read it in your countenance, Jacob!
Close, Jacob, and then—!'

JACOB.

Perhaps you'll give me another?

SILKY.

Well said, Jacob! You'll be a great man! Mind what I say to
you, and you'll be a great man! —Here's somebody coming!   40
Go, Jacob! Close!

JACOB.

And another guinea?   *Exit.*

SILKY.

This is a lucky stroke!

Enter Goldfinch.

So, Mr. Goldfinch? What do you want?

GOLDFINCH.

Money. A thousand pounds directly.   45

SILKY.

Fine talking, Mr. Goldfinch! Money's a scarce commodity!
Times are ticklish!

30. taken suddenly ill] suddenly
taken ill *MS*.

GOLDFINCH.

Tellee I must have it.

SILKY.

Give me but good security, and you know I'm your friend.

GOLDFINCH.

Yes; good security and fifty per cent!   50

SILKY.

Why, look you there now! For all you know, the last annuity
I had of you, I gave a full hundred more than was offered
by your friend Aaron, the Jew!

GOLDFINCH.

My friend? Your friend! You collogue together!

SILKY.

Hear you now! For all you know I have always been your   55
friend; always supplied you with money, have not I? And
when I saw you running to ruin, I never told you of it, did
I? I was willing to make all things easy!

GOLDFINCH.

Easy enough! You have pretty well eased me!

SILKY.

There is your companion, Jack Milford; I shall be a heavy   60
loser by him!

GOLDFINCH.

Ah! It's all up with poor Jack! He's fixed at last!

SILKY.

What do you mean?

GOLDFINCH.

Old Dornton has sent the Nabman after him!

SILKY.

And arrested him?   65

GOLDFINCH.

Yes, he's touched!

SILKY (*calling*).

Jacob!

Enter Jacob.

49. Give . . . friend] You know I'm   picious, Mr. Goldfinch; for all you
your friend. Give . . . friend *MS*.   know that I'm your friend! *MS*.
55. For . . . know] You are so sus-

54. *collogue*] intrigue, confer.
64. *Nabman*] police officer, constable.

Run as fast as you can to my good friend Mr. Strawshoe,
the attorney, and tell him to take out detainers for all the
debts I have bought up against Mr. Milford! Make haste!   70

JACOB.

Yes, sir.   *Exit.*

GOLDFINCH.

I thought you were Jack Milford's friend, too!

SILKY.

So I am, Mr. Goldfinch; but I must provide for my family!

GOLDFINCH.

Come, come! The bit! Tellee I want the coal, directly! Sale
at Tattersall's tomorrow morning! Three Pot8o's brood   75
mares with each an Eclipse colt! Would not lose 'em for all
Lombard Street! So will you let me have the bit?

SILKY.

Dear, dear! I tell you I can't, Mr. Goldfinch.

GOLDFINCH.

Then some other Jew must.

SILKY.

Jew! Hear you! Hear you! This it is to be the friend of an   80
ungrateful spendthrift! Calls me Jew! I, who go to morning
prayers every day of my life, and three times to tabernacle
on a Sunday!

GOLDFINCH.

Yes! You cheat all day, tremble all night, and act the
hypocrite the first thing in the morning.   *Going.*   85

SILKY.

Nay, but stay, Mr. Goldfinch! Stay! I want to talk to you!
I have a scheme to make a man of you!

GOLDFINCH.

What? Bind me 'prentice to a usurer?

68. my good friend] my friend *MS.*   *Q6, Q9–12.*
69. detainers] detainders *MS, Q4,*   75. Pot8o's] Herod *Q4, Q6, Q9–12.*

---

69. *detainers*] writs authorizing retention of a prisoner in custody at the
suit of another than the original creditor.

74. *bit, coal*] money.

75. *Pot8o's*] son of Eclipse, bred 1773, a great racer (said to have won
thirty-five of forty-six races) and a great stud.

77. *Lombard Street*] great London banking center.

SILKY.

Pshaw! You are in pursuit of the widow Warren?

GOLDFINCH.

Well? 90

SILKY.

Now what will you give me, and I'll secure her to you?

GOLDFINCH.

You?

SILKY.

I!

GOLDFINCH.

Which way?

SILKY.

I have a deed in my power, I won't tell you what, but I 95
have it, by which I can make her marry the man I please,
or remain a widow all her life; and that I am sure she will
never do if she can help it.

GOLDFINCH.

You a deed?

SILKY.

Yes, I. 100

GOLDFINCH.

Show it me!

SILKY.

Not for twenty thousand pounds! Depend upon me, I have it!
I tell you I'm your friend, and you shall have her! That is,
on proper conditions. If not, Mr. Goldfinch, you shall not
have her! 105

GOLDFINCH.

Indeed, old Judas! Well, what are your conditions?

SILKY.

I find the late alderman died worth a hundred and fifty
thousand pounds!

---

89. Pshaw! You] Pshaw! Will you
hear me, Mr. Goldfinch? You *MS*.
91. Now . . . you] The marriage
would set you up again! There
would be a foundation then, and I
could be your friend as formerly!
Now . . . you *MS*.

95. deed] instrument *MS*.
99. deed] instrument *MS*.
106. Indeed . . . conditions] Indeed,
old Judas! SILKY. She shall
marry the man I please! GOLD-
FINCH. Well . . . conditions] *MS*.

GOLDFINCH.

Ay?

SILKY.

Every farthing, Mr. Goldfinch! And my conscience tells me 110
that, risk and character and all things considered, I must
come in for my thirds.

GOLDFINCH.

Your conscience tells you that?

SILKY.

Yes, it does, Mr. Goldfinch. Fifty thousand is a fair price.

GOLDFINCH.

For the soul of a miser. 115

SILKY.

If you'll join me, say so.

GOLDFINCH.

Fifty thousand?

SILKY.

Not a farthing less! What, will there not be a hundred
thousand remaining?

GOLDFINCH.

Why, that's true! It will cut a fine dash! 120

SILKY.

To be sure it will! Come with me! I'll draw up a sketch of
an agreement. After which we must fight cunning. The
widow is a vain weak woman. You must get her written
promise!

GOLDFINCH.

Written? 125

SILKY.

Under her own hand; with a good round penalty in case of
forfeiture!

GOLDFINCH.

Well said, old one!

SILKY.

Not less than twenty thousand pounds! A jury would grant
half! 130

GOLDFINCH.

Why, you're a good one!

SILKY.

That would secure something, and we would snack!

GOLDFINCH.

Dammee, you're a deep one!

SILKY.

Ah, ha, ha, ha! Do you think I am, Mr. Goldfinch? Signed
on a stamp!   135

GOLDFINCH.

You know a thing or two!

SILKY.

Ah, ha, ha, ha! Do you think I do, Mr. Goldfinch?

GOLDFINCH.

You can teach 'em to bite the bubble!

SILKY.

Ah, ha, ha, ha! You joke, Mr. Goldfinch, you joke!

GOLDFINCH.

But the devil will have you at last!   140

SILKY.

Lord forbid, Mr. Goldfinch! Don't terrify me! I hate the
devil, Mr. Goldfinch; indeed I do! I hate the name of him!
Heaven keep me out of his fiery clutches!

GOLDFINCH.

No: he has you safe enough! Bait his trap but with a guinea,
and he is sure to find you nibbling!   145

SILKY.

Don't talk about the devil, Mr. Goldfinch! Pray don't! But
think about the widow; secure her.

GOLDFINCH.

I must have the coal though this evening?

SILKY.

Don't lose a moment, Mr. Goldfinch!

GOLDFINCH.

Must not lose the Eclipse colts!   150

---

150. Must . . . colts] I shall come   at home. Either the bit or I blow
again. Don't pretend you are not   you! Must . . . colts *MS*.

---

132. *snack*] share.
138. *bite the bubble*] swindle, cheat a fool.

SILKY.

> Pshaw, Mr. Goldfinch, think less of the colts and more of
> the widow! Get her promise in black and white!

Goldfinch going.

GOLDFINCH (turns).

> Tellee I must have 'em!

SILKY.

> All will then be safe!

GOLDFINCH.

> Must have 'em!   Exeunt. 155

ACT III

The house of the Widow Warren.
Jenny *and* Sophia *meeting.*

JENNY.

Oh, miss! I have got something for you!

SOPHIA.

Something for me! What is it? What is it?

JENNY (*her hand behind her*).

What will you give me?

SOPHIA (*feeling in her pocket*).

Oh, I'll give you—la, I've got no money! But I'll give you a
kiss and owe you sixpence.   5

JENNY.

No. A shilling without the kiss.

SOPHIA.

Well, well, a shilling.

JENNY (*giving her a small parcel*).

There then.

SOPHIA.

La! What is it? (*Reads.*) "To Miss Sophia Freelove."
And such a beautiful seal! It's a pity to break it. (*Opening*   10
the paper.) La! Nothing but a plumcake!

JENNY.

Is that all?

SOPHIA (*considering*).

Ecod! Ha, ha, ha, ha, ha! I do think—as sure as sixpence
it is! It is!

JENNY.

Is what?   15

SOPHIA.

Oh, la, it is!

JENNY.

What's the matter with the girl?

SOPHIA.

Ecod, Jenny, it is the most curious plumcake you ever saw!

JENNY.

I see nothing curious about it!

SOPHIA.

> Oh, but you shall see! Give me a knife! —Oh, no, that 20
> would spoil all! Look you, Jenny, look! Do but look!
> (*Breaks open the cake and finds a valentine.*) Ha, ha, ha, ha! I
> told you so! The sweet, dear—! (*Kisses it.*) Did you ever
> see such a plumcake in your whole life, Jenny? And look
> here! (*Opening the valentine.*) Oh, how beautiful! The 25
> shape of a honeysuckle! What should that mean? And two
> doves cooing! But here! Here's the writing.
>> "The woodbine sweet and turtledove
>> Are types of chaste and faithful love.
>> Ah! Were such peace and truth but mine, 30
>> I'd gladly be your valentine!"
> (*Repeating.*) "Were such peace and truth but mine!" La,
> now, Mr. Dornton, you know they are yours!

JENNY.

> So, so! Mr. Dornton sends you valentines, miss?

SOPHIA.

> Oh, yes, Jenny! He is the kindest, sweetest, handsomest 35
> gentleman!

JENNY.

> You must give me that valentine, miss.

SOPHIA.

> Give it you!

JENNY.

> Yes, that I may show it your mamma.

SOPHIA.

> Indeed but don't you think it! I would not give you this tiny 40
> bit of paper, no, not for a diamond as big—as big as the
> whole world! And if you were to tell ma, and she were to
> take it from me, I'd never love you, nor forgive you, as long
> as I live!

JENNY.

> Oh, but indeed, miss, I'm not obliged to keep secrets for 45
> nothing!

42. world! And] world! I would   *little finger.*) And *MS.*
sooner give you—here—I would   42. to tell . . . were] *om. Ox.*
sooner give you this! (*Holding up her*

SOPHIA.

Nah, Jenny, you know I am very good to you. And here!
Here! Don't tell ma, and I'll give you this silver thimble.

Exit Jenny.

Enter Widow Warren *and* Mr. Sulky.

WIDOW.

You are a very shocking person, Mr. Sulky! The wild man
of the woods broke loose! Do return to your keeper, good   50
orangutan; and don't go about to terrify children!

SULKY.

I tell you, madam, Mr. Milford is arrested.

SOPHIA.

My brother?

SULKY.

Locked up at a bailiff's in the next street.

SOPHIA.

Oh, dear!   55

WIDOW.

And pray now what is that to me?

SULKY.

Madam!

WIDOW.

I am not arrested.

SULKY.

Would you were!

WIDOW.

Oh, the savage!   60

SULKY.

The pitiless only should feel pain. The stonyhearted alone
should be enclosed by walls of stone.

SOPHIA.

Don't be cross with ma, sir; I'm sure she'll release my
brother.

WIDOW.

You are sure, minikin!   65

SOPHIA.

Yes, ma, for I am sure no soul on earth would suffer a

48. Don't tell ma, and] *om. MS.*

fellow creature to lie and pine to death, in a frightful dark dungeon, and fed with bread and water!

SULKY.

Your late husband recommended the payment of his son's debts. 70

WIDOW.

Recommended?

SULKY.

Yes.

WIDOW.

But leaving it to my own prudence.

SULKY.

More's the pity.

WIDOW.

Which prudence I shall follow. 75

SULKY.

It will be the first time in your life. You never yet followed prudence, you always ran before it.

SOPHIA.

Nay, come, dear ma, I am sure you have a pitiful heart! I am sure you could not rest in your bed if my poor brother was in prison! 80

WIDOW.

Hold your prattle, child!

SOPHIA.

Ah! I'm sure you'll make him happy, and pay his debts!

WIDOW.

Why, Jenny! *Calling.*

SULKY.

You won't?

WIDOW.

Jenny! 85

Enter Jenny.

SOPHIA.

La, dear sir, have patience.

SULKY.

You are an angel! —And you are—! *Exit.*

SOPHIA.

Nay, pray, sir, do stay! *Exit following.*

WIDOW.

I am glad the monster is gone! He is a very intolerable
person! Pray, Jenny, how did it happen that Mr. Dornton   90
went away without seeing me?

Enter Servant *and* Mr. Silky.

SERVANT.

Mr. Silky, madam.

WIDOW.

Leave us, Jenny.   *Exit* Jenny.

So, Mr. Silky. What is this very urgent business of yours?

SILKY (*looking round*).

Are we safe, madam? Will nobody interrupt us; nobody   95
overhear us?

WIDOW.

No, no. But what is the meaning of all this caution?

SILKY (*after fastening the door and carefully drawing the will from his
pocket*).

Do you know this handwriting, madam?

WIDOW.

Ah! It is my poor old dear man's, I see.

SILKY.

You have heard of a will he left in France?   100

WIDOW.

Pshaw! Will indeed? He left no will!

SILKY.

Yes, he did, madam.

WIDOW.

I won't believe it! He loved me too well to rob me of a single
guinea! Poor simple soul! I was his darling!

SILKY.

His darling, madam? With your permission, I will just read   105
a single clause in which his darling is mentioned! Look,
madam, it is the alderman's hand! (*Reads.*) "But as I
have sometimes painfully suspected the excessive affection
which my said wife, Winifred Warren, professed for me
during my decline, and that the solemn protestations she   110
made never to marry again, should she survive me, were
both done with sinister views, it is my will that, should she

marry, or give a legal promise of marriage, written or verbal,
that she shall be cut off with an annuity of six hundred a
year, and the residue of my effects in that case to be equally   115
divided between my natural son, John Milford, and my
wife's daughter, Sophia Freelove."

WIDOW.

Six hundred a year! An old dotard! To imagine that a
woman of my elegant ideas could exist on six hundred a
year! Brute! Monster! I hate him now as heartily as when   120
he was alive! But pray, sir, how came you by this will?

SILKY.

Why, it was odd enough! And yet easy enough! My name
is Silky, madam—

WIDOW.

Well?

SILKY.

And you know the executor's name is Sulky—   125

WIDOW.

Well?

SILKY.

The gentleman that delivered it only made a mistake of a
letter, and gave it to Mr. Silky instead of to Mr. Sulky!

WIDOW.

And where is that gentleman?

SILKY.

Ah, poor man! He is dead!   130

WIDOW.

Dead?

SILKY.

And gone! Was taken ill the very night he parted from me,
went to his hotel, was put to bed in a high fever, and carried
off in less than a week.

113–114. verbal, that] verbal, within
five years after my decease, that *MS.*
117. Freelove."] Freelove." You
see, madam? Signed by himself, and
witnessed? *MS.*
118–120. To imagine . . . year] *om.*
Inch., Ox.
132–134. Was . . . week] *om. Inch.,*

Ox.
134.] *After l. 134, MS prints:*
WIDOW. I have often heard that
you are a sad old rogue, Mr. Silky!
SILKY. Me, Madam? It was no
fault of mine! I did not so much as
recommend his apothecary! It was
merely a piece of good fortune!

WIDOW.

And does Mr. Sulky know of this will being delivered? 135

SILKY.

Not a syllable! It's all close and smooth! .

WIDOW.

So much the better. Come, give it me, and—

SILKY.

Excuse me there, madam! I can't do that!

WIDOW.

Why so?

SILKY.

My conscience won't let me! I must provide for my family! 140

WIDOW.

And pray what provision is this will to make for your family, Mr. Silky?

SILKY.

Why, madam, I have a proposal. You know the power of your own charms!

WIDOW.

Which I believe is more than you do, Mr. Silky. 145

SILKY.

Hah! Don't say so, madam! Don't say so! Would I were a handsome, rich and wellborn youth! But you know Mr. Goldfinch? Ah, ha, ha, ha! I could tell you a secret!

WIDOW.

What? That he is dying for me, I suppose?

SILKY.

Ah! So smitten! Talks of nothing else! 150

WIDOW.

And is that any secret, think you?

SILKY.

The alderman I find died worth more than a plum and a half—

WIDOW.

Well?

SILKY.

I have talked the matter over with my friend, Mr. Goldfinch, 155 and he thinks it but reasonable, that for a secret of so much

152. *a plum*] £100,000.

importance, which would almost sweep the whole away, I
should receive one third.

WIDOW.

Fifty thousand pounds, Mr. Silky?

SILKY.

I can't take less.   160

WIDOW.

Why, you are a greater rogue than even I thought you!

SILKY.

Lord, madam, it's no roguery! It's only a knowledge of the
world! A young husband with a hundred thousand pounds,
or poor six hundred a year without any husband!

WIDOW.

You are a very shocking old miser, Mr. Silky! A very repul- 165
sive sort of a person! What heart you had is turned to stone!
You are insensible of the power of a pair of fine eyes! But I
have made a conquest that places me beyond your reach—
I mean to marry Mr. Dornton!

SILKY (surprised).

What! Old Mr. Dornton, madam?   170

WIDOW.

Old Mr. Dornton, man? I never saw the figure in my life!
No! The gay and gallant young Mr. Dornton! The pride of
the city, and the lawful monarch of my bleeding heart!

SILKY.

Ha, ha, ha! Young Mr. Dornton!

WIDOW.

So you may take your will and light your fires with it! You 175
will not make a penny of it in any other way. Mr. Sulky, the
executor, is Mr. Dornton's partner, and when I marry Mr.
Dornton he will never inflict the absurd penalty.

SILKY.

Ha, ha, ha! No, madam! When you marry Mr. Dornton,
that he certainly never will! But if any accident should 180
happen to prevent the match, you will then let me hear
from you?

WIDOW.

Lord, good man! Don't mention the horrid idea! Do leave
me to my delightful meditations! I would indulge in soft
sensibility and dreams of bliss; and not be disturbed by dead 185

men's wills or the sordid extortions of an avaricious old
rogue!

SILKY.

Very well, madam! The secret for the present remains between ourselves! You'll be silent for your own sake! Only
remember, ha, ha, ha! If you should want me, I live at 190
Number 40. My name is on the door. Ha, ha, ha! Mr.
Dornton! Good morning, madam! Mr. Dornton! Ha, ha,
ha! You'll send if you should want me?   *Exit laughing.*

WIDOW (*calling*).

Jenny!

Enter Jenny.

JENNY.

Ma'am!   195

WIDOW.

As I was saying, Jenny, pray how did it happen that Mr.
Dornton went away without seeing me?

JENNY.

Indeed, ma'am, I don't know.

WIDOW.

Cruel youth!

JENNY.

I'm sure, ma'am, I wonder how you can like him better than 200
Mr. Goldfinch!

WIDOW.

Mr. Goldfinch is very well, Jenny. But Mr. Dornton! Oh,
incomparable!

JENNY.

I am sure, ma'am, if I was a rich lady, and a handsome lady,
and a fine lady, like you, I should say Mr. Goldfinch for my 205
money!

WIDOW.

Should you, Jenny? Well, I don't know—   *Languishing.*

GOLDFINCH (*without*).

Tellee I must see her.

188–189. remains between our-
selves] rests between you and me
MS.

203. incomparable] incomparable
youth *MS.*

WIDOW.

As I live, here he comes! He is such a boisterous person!
(*Goes to the glass.*)   How do I look, Jenny? I protest my face 210
is of all colors!

JENNY (*significantly after examining*).

You had better go up to your toilette for a minute.

WIDOW.

That smooth-tongued old extortioner has put me into such
a fluster—don't let him go, Jenny.

JENNY.

Never fear, ma'am.   215

WIDOW.

I'll not stay too long.   *Exit.*

Enter Goldfinch, *his clothes, hat, and boots dirtied by a fall.*

GOLDFINCH.

Here I am—all alive.

JENNY.

Dear! What's the matter?

GOLDFINCH.

Safe and sound! Fine kickup!

JENNY.

Have you been thrown?   220

GOLDFINCH.

Pitched five-and-twenty feet into a ditch. Souse!

JENNY.

Dear me!

GOLDFINCH.

Pretty commence! No matter—limbs whole—heart sound—
that's your sort!

JENNY.

Where did it happen?   225

GOLDFINCH.

Byroad—back of Islington—had them tight in hand too—
came to a short turn and a narrow lane—up flew a damned
dancing-master's umbrella—bounce—off they went—road
repairing—wheelbarrow in the way—crash—out flew I—

210–211. I protest ... colors] *om.*   214. fluster] flutter *Q4, Q6, Q9–12.
Ox.*

whiz—fire flashed—lay stunned—got up—looked foolish— 230
shafts broke—Snarler and Blackguard both down—Black-
and-all-black paying away, panels smashed, traces cut,
Snarler lamed.

JENNY.

Terrible!

GOLDFINCH.

Damned mad! Cursed a few, cut up Black-and-all-black, 235
horse-whipped Tom, took coach and drove here like a devil
in a whirlwind!

JENNY.

'Tis very well your neck's not broke!

GOLDFINCH.

Little stiff. No matter. Damn all dancing-masters and their
umbrellas!   240

JENNY.

You had better have been here, Mr. Goldfinch. You stand so
long, shilly-shally, that you'll be cut out at last. If you had
but a license now in your pocket, I'd undertake to have you
married in half an hour!

GOLDFINCH.

Do you think so?   245

JENNY.

Think? I'm sure on't.

GOLDFINCH.

Dammee, I'll post away and get one. Must not lose her; the
game's up if I do! Must have her! Be true to me, and I'll
secure you the hundred! I'll be back from the Commons in
a smack!   250

Enter the Widow Warren.

Ah! Widow! Here am I!

Runs up to her, kisses her boisterously, and dirties her clothes.

WIDOW (*looking at herself*).

I protest, Mr. Goldfinch! Was ever the like!

231. Snarler] Spanker *MS.*

---

249. *Commons*] Doctors' Commons, London, where the legal business
included licenses for marriage.
249–250. *in a smack*] instantly.

GOLDFINCH.

Never mind, brush off—I'm the lad! Been to Hatchet's.
Bespoke the wedding coach.

WIDOW.

But—sir—   255

GOLDFINCH.

Panels stripe painted—hammercloth fringed—green and
white—curtains festooned—patent wheels—silver furniture
—all flash—light as a bandbox—trundle and spin after my
greys like a tandem down hill—pass—show 'em the road
—whurr—whizzgig!—that's your sort!   260

WIDOW.

ꞌIt will be superb!

GOLDFINCH (with contempt).

Superb? Tellee it will be the thing! The go—the stare—the
gape—the gaze! The rich widow and the tight one! There
they go! Away they bowl! That's your sort!

WIDOW.

You have a taste for these things, Mr. Goldfinch!   265

GOLDFINCH.

Taste! Believe I have. Who more? Phaetons and curricles,
parks and pleasure grounds, up hill and down, highways
and byways—I'm the boy that shall drive you!

WIDOW.

Pardon me, Mr. Goldfinch; if a certain event were by the
wise disposition of Providence to take place, I should think 270
proper to drive.

GOLDFINCH.

You drive! If you do, damn me!

WIDOW.

Sir!

GOLDFINCH.

I'm christened and called Charles—Charles Goldfinch—
the knowing lad that's not to be had—winter and summer— 275
fair weather and foul—low ruts or no ruts—never take a

264. Away they bowl!] *om. Ox.*   *Inch., Ox.*
265–268. You ... byways] *om.*

---

253. *Hatchet's*] probably John Hatchett, the coachbuilder.
266. *curricle*] a light, two-wheeled carriage drawn by two horses abreast.

false quarter. No, no, widow—I drive. Hayait! Ah! Get on!
St—st—touch Whitefoot in the flank—tickle Snarler in the
ear—cut up the Yelper—take out a fly's eye—smack,
crack—that's your sort!   280

WIDOW.

I assure you, Mr. Goldfinch, you entertain very improper
suppositions concerning—

GOLDFINCH (*going*).

Go for the license—

WIDOW.

Nay, but surely, Mr.—

GOLDFINCH.

Go for the license. Resolved. Taken it here.   285

Pointing to his forehead.

WIDOW.

If retrospect and—and affection threw no other obstacles in
the way—yet the—the world—prudence.

GOLDFINCH.

The world! Prudence! Damn the world. Damn prudence.

WIDOW.

Oh, but, sir—

GOLDFINCH.

The world nor nobody else has nothing to do with neither   290
your prudence nor mine. We'll be married immediately—

WIDOW.

Immediately, Mr. Goldfinch! I—   *Undecided.*

GOLDFINCH.

What, you won't?

WIDOW.

Nay, Mr. Goldfinch, I—do not—absolutely renunciate—but
I—wish—   295

GOLDFINCH.

It was over—know you do—go for the license—

WIDOW.

Pray—dear Mr. Goldfinch—

GOLDFINCH.

Go for the license, I tellee.

WIDOW.

Only a word—

278. Whitefoot] Blackguard *MS*.

GOLDFINCH.

To the wise—I'm he—go for the license—that's your sort! 300

Exit.

WIDOW.

Mr. Goldfinch! I declare—   *Exit following.*

[III.ii]   *Scene changes to the house of Dornton.*
Mr. Dornton *and* Mr. Smith.

DORNTON.

Still the same hurry, the same crowd, Mr. Smith?

MR. SMITH.

Much the same, sir; the house never experienced a day like
this! Mr. Sulky thinks we shall never get through.

DORNTON.

Is Milford taken?

MR. SMITH.

Yes, sir.   5

DORNTON.

Unprincipled prodigal! My son owes his ruin to him alone.
But he shall suffer!

MR. SMITH.

My young master's tradesmen are waiting.

DORNTON.

Bid them come in.   *Exit* Mr. Smith.

All my own fault, my own fond folly! Denied him nothing, 10
encouraged him to spend; and now the unnatural father
can coolly think of turning him on the wide pitiless world;
there to starve, pine in a prison, rot in dungeons, among
agues, rheums, and loathsomeness!

Re-enter Mr. Smith *followed by* Tradesmen.

MR. SMITH.

This way, gentlemen!   15

DORNTON.

Zounds! What an army! —A vile, thoughtless profligate!
Yes, yes, misery be his portion; he merits it!

[III.ii]   someness *cancelled MS*; *om. Ox.*
11–14. and now . . . loathsomeness]   17. Yes . . . it]   *cancelled   MS*;   *om.*
om. Inch.; the unnatural . . . loath-   *Inch., Ox.*

–73–

Enter Servant.

SERVANT (*to* Mr. Dornton).

You are wanted in the countinghouse, sir.

DORNTON.

Very well. I'll be with you in a moment, gentlemen.
Abandoned spendthrift! *Exit, followed by* Mr. Smith. 20

FIRST TRADESMAN.

I don't like all this! What does it mean?

SECOND TRADESMAN.

Danger!

THIRD TRADESMAN.

He has been a good customer. None of your punctual pay-
masters, that look over their accounts.

FIRST TRADESMAN.

Oh, a different thing! Nothing to be got by them. Always 25
take care to affront them.

SECOND TRADESMAN.

Perhaps it is a trick of the old gentleman, to inspect into our
charges.

THIRD TRADESMAN.

I don't like that. Rather hear of any tax than of taxing my
bill. 30

FIRST TRADESMAN.

Humph! Tradesmen begin to understand these things, and
allow a reasonable profit!

SECOND TRADESMAN.

Can't have less than fifty per cent for retail credit trade!

THIRD TRADESMAN.

To be sure not, if a man would live in style, and save a
fortune as he ought. 35

FIRST TRADESMAN.

Hush! Mind—all devilish hard run!

OMNES.

Certainly!

FIRST TRADESMAN.

Not a guinea in the house! Tomorrow's Saturday—hem!

Re-enter Mr. Dornton.

DORNTON.

Your servant, gentlemen, your servant. Pray how happens it
that you bring your accounts in here? 40

FIRST TRADESMAN.
>We received notice, sir.

DORNTON.
>You have none of you any demands upon me?

FIRST TRADESMAN.
>Happy to serve you, sir.

SECOND TRADESMAN.
>We shall all be glad of your custom, sir.

OMNES.
>All, all!   45

DORNTON.
>And do you come expecting to be paid?

FIRST TRADESMAN.
>Money, sir, is always agreeable!

SECOND TRADESMAN.
>Tradesmen find it a scarce commodity!

THIRD TRADESMAN.
>Bills come round quick!

FOURTH TRADESMAN.
>Workmen must eat!   50

SECOND TRADESMAN.
>For my part, I always give a gentleman, who is a gentleman,
>his own time.

DORNTON.
>I understand you! —And what are you, sir, who seem to
>stand apart from the rest?

HOSIER.
>A hosier, sir. I am unworthy the company of these honest   55
>gentlemen, who live in style. I never affront a punctual
>paymaster, not I; and, what they will think strange, I get
>more by those who do look over their bills, than those who
>do not!

FIRST TRADESMAN.
>Humph!   60

SECOND TRADESMAN.   *Aside.*
>Blab!

THIRD TRADESMAN.
>Shab!

62. Shab] Scab *MS*.

___

62. *Shab*] sneak, low fellow.

DORNTON.

And what may be the amount of your bill, sir?

HOSIER.

A trifle, for which I have no right to ask.

DORNTON.

No right! What do you mean? 65

HOSIER.

Your son, sir, made me what I am; redeemed me and my
family from ruin; and it would be an ill requital of his
goodness to come here, like a dun, at such a time as this,
when I would rather, if that could help him, give him every
shilling I have in the world. 70

DORNTON (*greatly affected*).

Would you? Would you? You look like an honest man! But
what do you do here then?

HOSIER.

Mr. Dornton, sir, knew I should be unwilling to come, and
sent me word he would never speak to me more if I did not;
and, rather than offend him, I would even come here on a 75
business like this.

DORNTON (*shakes him by the hand*).

You are an honest fellow! An unaccountable—! And so
Harry has been your friend?

HOSIER.

Yes, sir, a liberal-minded friend, for he lent me money,
though I was sincere enough to tell him of his faults. 80

DORNTON.

Zounds, sir! How came you to be a weaver of stockings?

HOSIER.

I don't know, sir, how I came to be at all; I only know that
here I am.

DORNTON.

A philosopher!

HOSIER.

I am not fond of titles, sir—I'm a man. 85

DORNTON.

Why, is it not a shame, now, that the soul of Socrates should

77. unaccountable] honest unaccountable *MS.*

have crept and hid itself in the body of a stocking weaver?
Give me your bill!

HOSIER.

Excuse me, sir.

DORNTON.

Give me your bill, I tell you! I'll pay this bill myself.   90

HOSIER.

I cannot, must not, sir.

DORNTON.

Sir, I insist on—

Enter Harry Dornton.

So, sir! (*Turning angrily round.*) Why have you as-
sembled these people into whose debt you have dishonestly
run, wanting the power to pay, and who have as dis-   95
honestly trusted you, hoping to profit exorbitantly by your
extravagance?

HARRY.

Oh, sir, you don't know them! They are very complaisant,
indulgent kind of people. Are not you, gentlemen?

FIRST TRADESMAN.

Certainly, sir.   100

OMNES.

Certainly.

HARRY.

Be kind enough to wait a few minutes without, my very
good friends.   *Exeunt* Tradesmen.
Mr. Williams—   *Takes his hand.*

HOSIER.

Sir—   *Exit.* 105

DORNTON.

How dare you introduce this swarm of locusts here? How
dare you?

HARRY (*with continued good humor*).

Despair, sir, is a dauntless hero.

DORNTON.

Have you the effrontery to suppose that I can or shall pay
them? What is it you mean?   110

HARRY.

To let you see I have creditors.

DORNTON.

Cheats! Bloodsuckers!

HARRY.

Some of them, but that is my fault. They must be paid.

DORNTON.

Paid!

HARRY.

The innocent must not suffer for the guilty.   115

DORNTON.

You will die in an almshouse!

HARRY.

Maybe so, but the orphan's and the widow's curse shall not
meet me there!

DORNTON.

Harry! Zounds!   (*Checking his fondness.*)   Paid! Whom do
you mean to rob?   120

HARRY.

My name is Dornton, sir.

DORNTON.

Are you not—?   *Wanting words.*

HARRY.

Yes, sir.

DORNTON.

Quit the room! Begone!

HARRY.

You are the best of men, sir, and I—! But I hate whining. 125
Repentance is a pitiful scoundrel, that never brought back
a single yesterday. Amendment is a fellow of more mettle—
but it is too late. Suffer I ought, and suffer I must. My debts
of honor discharged, do not let my tradesmen go unpaid.

DORNTON.

You have ruined me!   130

HARRY.

The whole is but five thousand pounds!

DORNTON.

But? The counter is loaded with the destruction you have
brought upon us all!

HARRY.

No, no. I have been a sad fellow, but not even my extravagance can shake this house.   135

135. this] the *MS.*

Enter Mr. Smith, *in consternation.*

MR. SMITH.

Bills are pouring in so fast upon us we shall never get through!

HARRY (*struck*).

What! What is that you say?

MR. SMITH.

We have paid our light gold so often over that the people are very surly!   140

DORNTON.

Pay it no more! Sell it instantly for what it is worth, disburse the last guinea, and shut up the doors!

HARRY (*taking* Mr. Smith *aside*).

Are you serious?

MR. SMITH.

Sir!

HARRY (*impatiently*).

Are you serious, I say? Is it not some trick to impose upon   145
me?

MR. SMITH.

Look into the shop, sir, and convince yourself! If we have not a supply in half an hour we must stop!

HARRY (*wildly*).

Tol de rol—my father! Sir!   (*Turning away.*)   Is it possible?
Disgraced? Ruined? In reality ruined? By me? Are these   150
things so? —Tol de rol—

DORNTON.

Harry! How you look! You frighten me!

HARRY (*starting*).

It shall be done!

DORNTON.

What do you mean? Calm yourself, Harry!

HARRY.

Ay, by heaven!   155

---

139. *light gold*] below the standard or legal weight.

DORNTON.

Hear me, Harry!

HARRY (*going*).

This instant!

DORNTON (*calling*).

Harry!

HARRY (*returning*).

Don't droop! Don't despair! I'll find relief— (*Aside.*)
First to my friend— He cannot fail? But if he should! Why 160
ay, then to Megaera! I will marry her, in such a cause, were
she fifty widows, and fifty furies!

DORNTON.

Calm yourself, Harry!

HARRY.

I am calm! Very calm! —It shall be done! —Don't be de-
jected. You are my father. You were the first of men in the 165
first of cities, revered by the good and respected by the
great. You flourished prosperously! But you had a son! I
remember it!

DORNTON.

Why do you roll your eyes, Harry?

HARRY.

I won't be long away!   170

DORNTON (*catching his hand*).

Stay where you are, Harry! All will be well! I am very
happy! Do not leave me! I am very happy! Indeed I am,
Harry! Very happy!

HARRY.

Tol de rol—heaven bless you, sir! You are a worthy gentleman! I'll not be long!   175

DORNTON.

Hear me, Harry! I am very happy!

Enter a Clerk.

CLERK.

Mr. Smith, sir, desires to know whether we may send to the
Bank for a thousand pounds worth of silver.

---

161. *Megaera*] one of the three snaky-haired Furies.

HARRY (*furiously*).

No, scoundrel!   *Breaks away and exit.*

DORNTON (*calling and almost sobbing*).

Harry! Harry! I am very happy! Harry Dornton!   (*In a* 180
kind of stupor.)   I am very happy! Very happy!

Exit following.

[III.iii]   *Scene changes to the house of Mr. Silky.*
Mr. Silky *and* Jacob.

SILKY.

Mr. Goldfinch not called yet, Jacob?

JACOB.

No, sir.

SILKY.

Nor any message from the widow?

JACOB.

No, sir.   *Knocking heard.*

SILKY.

See who knocks, Jacob!   *Exit* Jacob.   5
I dare say it is one or t'other! They must come to me at last!

Enter Harry Dornton *in wild haste, following* Jacob.

HARRY (*entering*).

Are you sure he is at home?

JACOB.

He is here, sir.   *Exit.*

HARRY (*panting*).

Mr. Silky—!

SILKY.

Ah! My dear Mr. Dornton, how do you do? I hope you are   10
very well! I am exceedingly glad to see you! This call is so
kind, so condescending! It gives me infinite pleasure!

HARRY.

Mr. Silky, you must instantly grant me a favor!

SILKY.

A favor! What is it? How can I serve you? I would run to
the world's end.   15

[III.iii]   Pray, sir, be seated! Sit, sir, I
11. you! This] you! Here chairs!   beseech you! This *MS.*

HARRY.

> You must exert your whole friendship!

SILKY.

> Friendship, sir? Say duty! 'Twas you that made a man of
> me! I should have been ruined, in the Bench, I know not
> where or what, had you not come forward and supported
> me at the critical moment! And now I can defy the world!   20

HARRY (*impatiently*).

> Hear me! I know you can.

SILKY.

> Oh, yes! The sum you lent me, a lucky speculation, five years
> of continual good fortune, and other little lifts have made
> me—! I won't say what. But, your father and perhaps
> another or two excepted, I say perhaps, I'll show my head   25
> with the proudest of 'em.

HARRY.

> Why then I am a fortunate man!

SILKY.

> To be sure you are! How can I serve you? What can I do?
> Make me happy!

HARRY.

> You can rescue me from frenzy!   30

SILKY.

> Can I? I am proud! Infinitely happy! What? How? I am
> a lucky fellow! Tell me which way? Where can I run?
> What can I do?

HARRY (*dreading*).

> The request is serious—trying!

SILKY.

> So much the better! So much the better! Whom would I   35
> serve, if not you? You! The son of the first man in the city!

HARRY (*wildly*).

> You mistake!

SILKY.

> I don't! You are, you are! Dornton and Company may
> challenge the world, the house of Hope perhaps excepted!

27. fortunate] happy *MS*.

---

18. *Bench*] King's Bench Prison for debtors and criminals.
39. *Hope*] a wealthy, long established, Amsterdam banking family.

HARRY.

Woefully mistake!   40

SILKY.

Pooh!

HARRY.

Our house is in danger of stopping payment!

SILKY.

Sir? Stop payment!

HARRY.

My follies are the cause!

SILKY.

Stop payment?   45

HARRY.

I have not been used to ask favors—but—

SILKY.

Stop payment!

HARRY.

Scorn me, curse me, spurn me, but save my father!

SILKY.

Stop payment?

HARRY.

What means this alteration in your countenance?   50

SILKY.

Oh, dear, no! Ha, ha, ha! Not in the least! Ha, ha, ha, I
assure you, I, I, I—

HARRY.

I have told you our situation. Yourself and two other friends
must jointly support my father, by your credit, to the
amount of fifty thousand pounds. Mark me! Must!   55

SILKY.

Fifty thousand pounds, Mr. Dornton! Fifty thousand
pounds! Are you dreaming? Me? Fifty thousand pounds!
Me? Or half the sum? Or a fifth of the sum? Me!

HARRY.

Prevaricating scound——! Hear me, sir!

SILKY (*in fear*).

Yes, sir!   60

HARRY.

I must be calm— (*Bursting out.*)   Are you not a—! I say—
sir—you have yourself informed me of your ability, and I

must insist, observe, sir! I insist on your immediate performance of this act of duty!

SILKY.

Duty, and fifty thousand pounds! Are you mad, Mr.   65
Dornton? Are you mad? Or do you think me mad?

HARRY.

I think you the basest of wretches!

SILKY.

Nay, Mr. Dornton, I would do anything to serve you! Anything, I protest to Heaven! Would go anywhere, run—

HARRY.

Of my errands, wipe my shoes! Any dirty menial office that   70
cost you nothing. And this you call showing your gratitude?

SILKY.

Is it not, Mr. Dornton?

HARRY (*his anger rising*).

And will you give no help to the house?

SILKY.

Nay, Mr. Dornton—!

HARRY.

After the favors you have been for years receiving, the   75
professions you have been daily making, and the wealth
you have by these means been hourly acquiring! Will you
not, sir?

SILKY (*retreating*).

Nay, Mr. Dornton—!

HARRY.

Will you not, sir?   80

SILKY.

Don't hurt a poor old man! I can't!

HARRY (*seizing, shaking him, and throwing him from him*).

Scoundrel!   *Exit.*

SILKY.

Bless my heart! Stop payment? The house of Dornton!
Fifty thousand pounds? I declare I am all of a tremble!
James! William!   85

Enter two Clerks.

Have we any bills on the house of Dornton?

85. James] Jacob *MS*, *Ox*. For the   of the First Clerk are assigned to
remainder of the scene, the speeches   Jacob in *MS* and *Ox*.

FIRST CLERK.

I have just been examining the books, sir. We have bills to
the amount of—

SILKY.

How much? How much? A thousand pounds?

FIRST CLERK.

Three, sir.   90

SILKY.

Three! Three thousand? Bless my heart!

FIRST CLERK.

We heard the news the very moment after young Mr.
Dornton came in!

SILKY.

Run, pay the bills away!

FIRST CLERK.

Where, sir?   95

SILKY.

Anywhere! Anybody will take 'em! Run with them to my
dear friend, Mr. Smallware; it is too far for him to have
heard of the crash. Begone! Don't leave him! Give my very
best respects to him! He will oblige me infinitely! Fly!

Exit First Clerk.

And go you, James, to the clearing house, and get it whis- 100
pered among the clerks. Then, if there are any of Dornton's
bills to be bought at fifty per cent discount, let me know. I
will buy up all I can—   *Exit* Clerk.
It's a safe speculation; I know the house; there must be a
good round dividend.   *Exit.* 105

ACT IV

The house of the Widow Warren.

Enter Jenny *followed by* Harry Dornton, *who with an oppressed heart, but half drunk with wine and passion, assumes the appearance of wild and excessive gaiety.*

HARRY.

    Away, handmaid of Hecate! Fly!

JENNY.

    Lord, sir, you don't mean as you say!

HARRY.

    Will you begone, Cerberea? Invite my goddess to descend in a golden shower, and suddenly relieve these racking doubts.   5

JENNY.

    Goddess! I knew you meant Miss Sophy!

HARRY.

    Prime tormentrix to the Furies, begone!

JENNY.

    What, sir, to my old mistress?

HARRY.

    Hear you? Yes! I want an old mistress, with her old gold, instantly to relieve an injured old man—tol de rol—   10 Vanish, daughter of Nox! Tell her what a gay and lovesick humor I am in—tol de rol.

Enter Widow, *and exit* Jenny, *dissatisfied.*

WIDOW (*smiling*).

    Mr. Dornton!

HARRY.

    Widow! Here am I! Phaeton the second hurled from my flaming car! I come burning with fierce desires, devoutly   15 bent on committing the deadly sin of matrimony! May these things be? Speak, my saving angel!

6–13.] *om. Inch.*   7–13.] *om. Ox.*

---

   3. *Cerberea*] Harry Dornton's coinage from Cerberus, the three-headed dog of Hades.

WIDOW.

Fie upon you! How can you throw one into such an in-
superable trepidation of spirits?

HARRY.

Will you have me? Pronounce but the blessed Yes, and I am   20
thine forever and for aye.

WIDOW.

Dear Mr. Dornton—! You—I—

HARRY.

Ay, ay, I know very well. The formal No, the crimson blush,
the half-consenting side-glance, the hesitating Yes, the
palpitation violent—we'll suppose them all—there, there!   25
I have acted them over, and the parson's tragical farce is
going to begin!

WIDOW.

Nay, but—! Dear Mr. Dornton—!

HARRY.

Do not imagine, amiable widow, that I am mad! No, no,
no! (*With a hysteric laugh.*) Only a little flighty. Left my   30
father furiously, drank three bottles of Burgundy frantically,
flew in amorous frenzy to the attack, and will carry the
place or die on the spot! Powder and poison await my
choice; and let me tell you, sweet widow, I am a man of
my word. So you'll have me, won't you?   35

WIDOW.

Oh, Mr. Dornton—!

HARRY.

Why, you would not see my father perish! Would you?
And me expire! Would you?

WIDOW.

Am I so very cruel?

HARRY.

Then say Yes! Yes or—pistols—daggers—cannon balls!   40

WIDOW.

Yes, sir, yes, yes!

HARRY.

Hold, fair widow! Kind widow, hold! Be not rash! I am the
veriest villain! Avoid me! A ruined—! But that were indeed

18–27.] *om. Inch., Ox.*

a trifle—my father! Him! Him have I ruined! Heard you
that? Bring forth your hoards! Let him once more be him- 45
self, and bid me kiss the dust!

WIDOW (*aside*).

Elegant youth! (*Aloud.*) Ah, you flatterer! I own you
have been a little—wild, but—

HARRY.

A little! Oh! Ha, ha, ha! Widow, I am a sad fellow! A
damned sad dog! I tell you I have ruined my father—a 50
prince of fathers! Who, had I not been a rascal, would have
given me his soul! And I have ruined him! Ruined him!
Beware of me! Fly me! —Yet should you? Rise, imps of
night! Deep have I sworn to find some means to save a
father from destruction, and I will keep my oath though—! 55

WIDOW.

Oh, fie! How can you terrify one so?

HARRY (*eagerly*).

And wilt thou, widow, be his support? Wilt thou?

WIDOW.

Cruel question! How can I deny?

HARRY.

Immortal blessings be upon thee! My father!

WIDOW.

Will be all rapture to hear—! 60

HARRY.

Will he? Words of comfort! Will he? A buxom, fair and
bounteous dame, whose treasures can restore his tottering
fortunes to their wonted splendor! Ha! Will he? Will he?

WIDOW.

Certainly, Mr. Dornton, he cannot be displeased at such a
choice. 65

HARRY (*shakes his head*).

Ah, ha, ha, ha! (*Sighs.*) You don't know my father! A
strange, affectionate—! That loves me—! Oh! He—! And
you see how I use him! You see how I use him! But no
matter—tol de rol— We'll be married tonight.

47–55.] *om. Inch.*   Rise *MS.*
47–56. Ah . . . so] *om. Ox.*   61–65.] *cancelled MS*; *om. Inch., Ox.*
53. you? Rise] you? Should you?

WIDOW.

> Oh, fie!   70

HARRY.

> Ay, my madonna! Tonight's the day—the sooner the
> better! 'Tis to rescue a father, blithesome widow! A father!
> To save him have I fallen in love—remember—sin with
> open eyes, widow—money—I must have money—early in the
> morn, ere counters echo with the ring of gold, fifty thousand   75
> must be raised!

WIDOW.

> It shall, Mr. Dornton.

HARRY.

> Why, shall it? Shall it? Speak again, beatific vision, speak!
> Shall it?

WIDOW.

> Dear Mr. Dornton, it shall.   80

HARRY.

> Tol de rol—he shall live! He shall smile! Again his heart
> shall feel joy! Oh, my bland and bonny widow!
>
> > *Partly singing.*
>
> *My widow fair and debonair—*
> Keep thy word— Let but my father be himself, and I am
> thine! Body and soul thine!   85

WIDOW (*coquettishly*).

> And are you really—? Oh, no! No—you are not in love?

HARRY.

> Fathom and half, poor Tom!   *Singing and sighing.*
> > *And we'll love by day, and we'll live by night—*
> > *With a hey and a ho and a heigho, widow!*
> I have drunk Burgundy—to your health, auspicious   90
> Amazon! —Burgundy!   *Sings.*
> > *For I wanted the grace*
> > *Of a bold villain's face,*
> > *To prevail, with heigho,*
> > *On a buxom widow.*   *Kisses her.*   95

81–85. he . . . thine] *cancelled MS.*   81–99. Tol . . . saved] *om. Ox.*;
                                            he . . . saved *om. Inch.*

---

87. *King Lear*, III.iv.37.

WIDOW (*coquetting*).

    Fie! I shall hate you, if you are so fond of me! I shall indeed!
But no—you are man! Roving, faithless man!

HARRY.

    No, no! Fear not! Thou, gracious widow, art my overflowing
cup of consolation. What! A father saved? Remember!
Fifty thousand the first thing in the morning?   100

WIDOW (*still coquetting*).

    And would not a part this evening—?

HARRY (*suddenly.*)

    What sayest thou? Oh, no! Whoo! Thousands—

WIDOW.

    No. You are a naughty bad man, and I don't love you; I
don't indeed. Else I have a trifling sum.

HARRY (*eagerly*).

    How much?   105

WIDOW.

    Six thousand.

HARRY.

    Six?

WIDOW.

    Which I meant to have disposed of, but—

HARRY.

    No, no! I'll dispose of it, dear widow! (*Kisses her.*) I'll
dispose of it in a twinkling! (*Elated.*) Thou art my 110
goddess! By the faith of my body but I will thank thee—
yea, thee will love exceedingly!   *Kisses her again.*

WIDOW (*languishingly*).

    Oh, fie! No, you won't! Will you?

HARRY (*sighs*).

    Will I? Shall I not be in duty bound?

WIDOW (*more fondly*).

    No! You can't love me.   115

HARRY.

    Ha, ha, ha! My fair Pelican of Potosi! Queen of Pactolus!

98. No, no] *om. MS.*   110–116. Thou ... Pactolus] *om*
103–104. No . . . Else] *om. Inch., Ox.*   *Inch., Ox.*

   116. *Potosi*] city and district in Bolivia, once the world's richest source of
silver.
   116. *Pactolus*] river in Asia Minor which yielded gold-bearing sand.

Doubt not my gratitude. Let this and this—   *Kissing.*
WIDOW.

Fie! You are a sad man—but I'll bring you a draft!
HARRY.

Do, my blooming widow! Empress of the golden isles, do!
WIDOW.

I tell you, you are a very bad man! —But remember, this   120
trifle is for your own use.
HARRY (*self-indignation*).

No, my pearl unparalleled! My father's! My father's! My
pocket is an insidious gulf, into which I never more will
guineas cast. Save but my father, and I will kiss the ground
on which thou treadest, and live and breathe but on thy   125
bounty.   *Exit* Widow.

>   At least till time and fate shall means afford
>   Somewhat to perform, worthy of man and me.

Enter Jenny, *peeping.*

JENNY.

St!
HARRY.

Ah, ha! My merry maid of May!   130
JENNY.

I suppose you are waiting to see Miss Sophy, now you have
got rid of the old lady?
HARRY.

Got rid of the old lady? Thou brazen pin-placer! Thou
virgin of nine-and-twenty years' occupation! No. I have not
got rid of the old lady! The old lady is to be my blooming,   135
youthful bride! And I, happy youth, am written and des-
tined in the records of eternity her other half! Before the
stars were this marriage was decreed! Heigho!
JENNY.

Lord, sir, what rapturation! But stay a little, and I'll tell
Miss Sophy her mamma wants her, here; so then—hush!— 140

120. I . . . man] *om. Ox.*   133–135. Thou brazen . . . lady]
122–124. My father's! My pocket   *om. Inch.*
. . . cast] *om. Inch.*; My pocket . . . 137–138. Before . . . decreed] *can-*
cast *om. Ox.*   *celled MS; om. Inch., Ox.*

Jenny *retires, making a sign, and re-enter the* Widow Warren.

WIDOW.

An't you a sad man? Here's the draft.

HARRY.

Thanks, my Sultana! Thou shalt find me very grateful. Thou
hast bought and paid for me, and I am thine! By fair and
honest traffic thine! This halcyon night the priest, pro-
nouncing conjurations dire—   145

WIDOW.

Fie! I won't look at you!

HARRY.

Ay, tonight we'll marry; shall we not?

WIDOW.

I'll not answer you a word!

        Enter Sophia *skippingly, but stops short.*

You are a dangerous man! (*Sitting down and coquetting.*)
How dare you talk to me of tonight?   150

HARRY.

Tonight shall be a night of wonder! And we'll love like—
[*aside*] like Darby and Joan!

WIDOW (*languishingly*).

I shall hate you intolerably!   Sophia *advancing on tiptoe.*

HARRY.

Hey for the parson's permission! Hey, my sublime widow!

WIDOW.

To steal thus upon one at an unguarded moment—!   155

HARRY.

But here first let me kneel, and thus to Ceres pay—
      Going to kiss her hand in rapture, meets the eye of Sophia.

WIDOW.

I'll never forgive you! I hate you now worse than ever.

SOPHIA (*coming between them with bursting trepidation, taking the valentine
from her bosom and presenting it*).

There, sir!

---

141. An't ... man] *cancelled MS*;   Fie *MS.*
om. Inch., Ox.   149. You ... man] *om. Inch.*
142–144. Thou shalt ... traffic   148–150. *om. Ox.*
thine] *om. Inch., Ox.*   157.] *om. Inch., Ox.*
146. Fie] Tonight, Mr. Dornton?

WIDOW.

> Ah!

SOPHIA.

> There, sir! —Oh, pray, sir, take it, sir!   160

WIDOW.

> Why, minikin—!

SOPHIA.

> I request, sir! I desire, sir!

HARRY (*declining it*).

> Tol de rol—

SOPHIA (*tearing the paper piecemeal, and throwing it spitefully away*).

> Why, then there, sir—and there, sir—and there, there,
> there, sir!   165

WIDOW.

> Poor minikin! I declare, she is jealous!

SOPHIA (*her sobs rising*).

> And I'll—I'll—write to my—to my grandma-a-a-a directly—

WIDOW.

> Fie, child!

SOPHIA.

> And I'll go do-o-o-own—into Glo-o-o-ostershire—

WIDOW.

> Go up to your chamber, child!   170

SOPHIA.

> And I'll tell my grandma what a false, base, bad man you
> are; and she shall ha-ate you, and despise you; and every-
> body shall ha-ate you, and despise you; and I'll ha-a-ate
> you, and despise you myself!

WIDOW.

> Poor thing!   175

SOPHIA.

> And moreover I'll hate and despise all mankind! And for
> your sake [*with great energy*] I'll live and die a maid!

WIDOW.

> Yes, child, that I dare be sworn you will!

HARRY.

> Widow! I'm a sad fellow! Don't have me—I'm a vile

172–173. and everybody ... despise you;] *om. Q12, Inch., Ox.*

fellow! Sophy! You are right to despise me! I am going to 180
marry your mother!

SOPHIA.

I'll go down into Glo-o-oostershire—I wo-on't live in such a
falsehearted city! And you ought to be ashamed of yourself,
ma, to make yourself so ridiculous!

HARRY.

No, no, sweet sylph, it is my fault! All my fault!   185

WIDOW (*enraged*).

Begone, miss!

HARRY (*interposing*).

Sweet widow! Gentle widow! —I've sold myself, Sophy!
Six thousand pounds is the earnest money paid down, for
the reptile Harry Dornton! —I love you, Sophy!

WIDOW.

How, Mr. Dornton?   190

HARRY.

I do, by heaven! Take back your money, widow! (*Offering
the draft.*)   I'm a sad scoundrel!

SOPHIA.

You are a base faithless man, you know you are! And you
are a pitiless woman, a merciless woman, for all you are my
own mother, to let my poor brother Milford go to be starved 195
to death in a dark dungeon!

HARRY.

Milford in prison?

SOPHIA.

Yes, sir; arrested by your cruel, old, ugly father! I'm sure he
is ugly! Though I never saw him in my life, I'm sure he is an
ugly, hideous, ugly monster!   *Exit.* 200

HARRY.

Is this true, widow?

185.] *After l. 185, MS prints*:
SOPHIA. But she'll comb your
hair! She'll give you your creepings!
192.] *After l. 192, MS prints*:
SOPHIA. You might be ashamed
of yourself to throw your money
away, upon a falsehearted, good for

nothing, vile deceiver, that will
laugh at you and bring you home a
madam under your very nose!
WIDOW. Would you, Mr. Dornton? HARRY. No, widow, no; I
think not. I'm a sad fellow, but I
think I would not do that.

WIDOW (*stammering*).

Sir—

HARRY (*agitated*).

Arrested by my father? —Squandering her money on a
ruined reprobate, and won't release her husband's son?

WIDOW.

Nay, but, dear Mr. Dornton! 205

HARRY.

I'll be with you again presently, widow; presently, presently.

Exit.

WIDOW (*speaking after him*).

Tonight, you know, Mr. Dornton—?

Enter Jenny.

JENNY.

Mr. Goldfinch is coming up, ma'am.

WIDOW.

I have no time to waste with Mr. Goldfinch. I'll presently
send him about his business. Mr. Dornton talks I don't 210
know how, Jenny—says it must be tonight.

Enter Goldfinch.

GOLDFINCH.

Well, widow?

WIDOW (*walks up the stage disdainfully*).

Not so free, sir!

JENNY (*aside to* Goldfinch).

Have you got the license?

GOLDFINCH.

No. 215

JENNY.

No!

GOLDFINCH.

No. Been to Tattersall's.

JENNY.

And not for the license?

GOLDFINCH.

Tellee I've been to Tattersall's!

207.] *om. Inch.*

JENNY.

Ah! It's all over! 220

GOLDFINCH.

Made sure of the Eclipse colts! Must not lose 'em!

JENNY (*aside*).

Stupid booby!

WIDOW (*advancing*).

What is your present business, sir?

GOLDFINCH.

My business? Ha, ha, ha! That's a good one! I'll tell you
my business— *Approaching with open arms.* 225

WIDOW (*haughtily*).

Keep your distance, sir!

GOLDFINCH.

Distance, widow? No, that's not the way. I should be
double distanced if I did.

WIDOW.

Were you indeed a man of deportment and breeding—!

GOLDFINCH.

Breeding? Look at my spurs! 230

WIDOW.

Had you the manner, the spirit, the—! But no— You are no
gentleman.

GOLDFINCH (*claps on his hat and takes a lounging impudent swagger*).

Whew! No gentleman? Dammee that's a good one! Charles
Goldfinch no gentleman? Ask in the box lobby! Enquire at
the school! *In a boxing attitude.* 235

WIDOW.

Sir, you are a tedious person; your company is troublesome!

GOLDFINCH.

Turf or turnpike, keep the best of cattle. Walk, trot or
gallop—run, amble or canter—laugh at everything on the
road—give 'em all the go-by—beat the trotting butcher!
Gentleman? That's your sort! 240

JENNY (*aside to* Goldfinch).

Follow me. *Exit.*

WIDOW.

I beg, sir, I may not be intruded upon with you or your
horse jockey jargon any more. *Exit.*

236. Sir . . . person] *om. MS.*

-96-

GOLDFINCH.

Here's a kickup. What's all this? Must have her or smash!
Smirker [*pointing after* Jenny] will tell me what it means. 245
Smart thing for a lightweight. Spirit, shape, and form—
carry a fine neck in a running martingale—shows blood—
win all the give and takes—take her into training—match
her the Abingdon mile against all England—that's your
sort! *Exit.* 250

[IV.ii]

Scene changes to an apartment at the house of a Sheriff's Officer. Enter
Harry Dornton *in the same hurry and* Officer.

HARRY.

Dispatch, man! Dispatch! Tell Jack Milford I can't wait a
moment! —Hold! —Write an acquittal instantly for the
thousand pounds. But say not a word to him of my intention!

OFFICER.

A thousand, sir? It is almost five thousand!

HARRY.

Impossible! 5

OFFICER.

There are detainers already lodged to that amount.

HARRY.

Five thousand?

OFFICER.

Must I write the acquittal for the sum total?

HARRY.

No. —Yes, write it however. Have it ready. Early tomorrow
morning it shall all be paid. 10

OFFICER.

In the meantime there may be more detainers.

244–250. What's ... sort] *cancelled MS*; *om. Inch.*; —dish'd again—I knew I should have no luck— started badly in the morning— d—n all dancing masters and their umbrellas *Ox.*

248. *give and takes*] a racing prize in which the horses carry weights varying according to their heights.
249. *Abingdon mile*] on the Newmarket racecourse; however, there was also a race meeting on the Common at Abingdon, Berkshire, of about a mile in length, at least as early as 1733 and continuing until 1875.

HARRY.

> Damnation! What shall I do? —Run, send him! And do you
> hear, a bottle of champagne and two rummers! —Rummers!
> Mind! —Not a word to him!　　　　　　　*Exit* Officer.
> Five thousand? And more detainers!　　　　　　　　15

Enter Waiter with bottle and glasses, and Milford *following.*

MILFORD.

> Mr. Dornton!

HARRY.

> How now, Jack! What's your wonder? I can't stay a
> moment with you, but I could not pass without giving you
> a call. Your hand, my boy! Cheer up!

MILFORD.

> Excuse me, sir!　　　　　　　　20

HARRY.

> Why, Jack! Pshaw! Cast away this gloom and be—Honest
> Jack Milford! You are now in tribulation; what of that?
> Why, man, the blessed sun himself is sometimes under a
> cloud! Wait but till tomorrow. —Where is this wine?
> (*Fills the rummers.*) Come, drink, and wash away grief!　25
> 'Sblood, never look frosty and askance, man, but drink,
> drink, drink!

MILFORD (*abruptly*).

> Sir? I am not disposed to drink!

HARRY.

> Why, what a tabernacle phrase is that! Here's confusion to
> all sorrow and thinking! —I could a tale unfold—! But I　30
> won't afflict you. I must fly, yet I can do no good tonight—
> Hurrah, Jack! Keep up your spirits! Be determined, like
> me! I am the vilest of animals that crawl the earth, yet I
> won't flag! I'll die a bold-faced villain! I have sold myself—
> am disinherited—have lost—ah, Sophia! Hurrah, Jack!　35

21–24. Pshaw . . . tomorrow] *om.*　*Ox.*
Inch.　　　　　　　　　　　　29. Why . . . that] *om. Inch., Ox.*
24. this wine] the wine *Q12, Inch.,*　　31. I must . . . tonight] *om. Inch.*

---

13. *rummers*] large glasses, especially for wine.
29. *tabernacle phrase*] Puritanic.
30. *I could . . . unfold*] *Hamlet,* I.v.15.

Keep it up! Round let the great globe whirl; and whirl it
will, though I should happen to slide from its surface into
infinite nothingness. Drink, my noble soul!

MILFORD.

Your mirth is impertinent, sir!

HARRY.

So it is, Jack, damned impertinent! But ruin is around us,   40
and it is high time to be merry!

MILFORD.

Sir? I must inform you that, though I have been betrayed
by you and imprisoned by your father, I will not be insulted!

HARRY.

Betrayed by me?

MILFORD.

Ay, sir! I have had full information of your mean arts! It   45
was necessary I should be out of the way, that your designs
on Mrs. Warren might meet no interruption!

HARRY.

Pshaw! Good day, Jack, good day!

MILFORD.

And pray, sir, inform your father I despise his meanness,
and spurn at his malice!   50

HARRY (*suddenly returning and darting on him, but stopping short*).

Jack Milford! Utter no blasphemy against my father! I am
half mad! I came your friend—

MILFORD.

I despise your friendship!

HARRY.

That as you please. Think all that is vile of me—I defy you
to exceed the truth—but utter not a word against my father!   55

MILFORD.

Deliberately, pitifully malignant! Not satisfied with the
little vengeance he himself could take, he has sent round to
all my creditors!

HARRY.

'Tis false!

MILFORD.

False?   60

HARRY.

A vile, eternal falsehood!

Enter Officer *with papers and writs.*

OFFICER.

Gentlemen! Did you call?

HARRY (*interrupting him*).

Leave the room, sir!

OFFICER.

But—!

HARRY.

We are busy, sir!   65

OFFICER.

I thought—!

HARRY.

I tell you we are busy, and must not be interrupted!

Exit Officer.

Pause of consideration.

Mr. Milford, you shall hear from me immediately.

Exit Harry.

MILFORD (*after ruminating*).

What were those papers? Surely I have not been rash?
Nobody but his father could have brought my creditors thus   70
on me all at once? He seemed half drunk or half frantic!
Said he was ruined, disinherited. Talked something of
tomorrow. What could the purport of his coming be?

Enter Officer.

Well, sir?

OFFICER.

Here is a note, sir.   75

MILFORD.

From whom?

OFFICER.

The young gentleman.

MILFORD (*reads aside*).

"I understand you are at liberty—" How! At liberty?
(*The* Officer *bows.*) (*Reads.*) "I shall walk up to Hyde
Park: you will find me at the Ring at six—exactly at six"—   80
At liberty?

---

80. *the Ring*] a circular course in Hyde Park, used for riding and driving.

OFFICER.

Your debts are all discharged.

MILFORD.

Impossible! Which way? By whom?

OFFICER.

Why, sir—that is—

MILFORD.

No hesitation, but tell me by whom?   85

OFFICER.

Sir, I thought I perceived some anger between you and the young gentleman?

MILFORD.

Ask no questions, sir; make no delays! Tell me who has paid my debts? Tell me the truth. Consequences you do not suspect depend upon your answer!   90

OFFICER.

I perceive, sir, there has been some warmth between you; and though the young gentleman made me promise silence and secrecy—

MILFORD (*astonishment*).

What, then it was Mr. Dornton? (Officer *bows*.) Madman! What have I done!   *Exeunt.*   95

[IV.iii]   *Scene changes to the house of Dornton.*
          Enter Harry Dornton, *followed by* Mr. Smith.

HARRY.

And the danger not yet past?

MR. SMITH.

Far from it! Mr. Sulky has twice brought us supplies, and is gone a third time.

HARRY.

Brave spirit! He would coin his heart! —My father supports it nobly?   5

MR. SMITH.

He is anxious only for you.

HARRY.

Well, well! Ha, ha, ha! Tol lol—I'll bring him relief. Comfort him, assure him of it! —Ay, hear me heaven and—!

Tonight it is too late, but tomorrow all shall be well!
Excellent well!   10

MR. SMITH (*significantly*).

You will marry the widow?

HARRY.

Have you heard? Ay, boy, ay! We'll marry! I will go and
prepare her. We'll marry! Early in the morning that all
may be safe.

MR. SMITH.

Will that be right?   15

HARRY.

I have told her the truth. She knows all; knows what a vile
infernal—I tell you she knows me! My father again shall
look upon the glare of day! First to the proctor, next to the
lawyer, and then—! Ha, ha, ha! Ay, then to my fair bride!
Hearest thou, my noble soul? I say my bride! My fair, my   20
blooming, thrice-bedded bride! No novice she, old true
blue! Tol de rol— It will be a merry wedding! Console my
father! Cheer him! Enlighten his soul with hope! I'll keep
my word! What, does he not know me! Am I not his own
son? Why, ay— (*Looking at his watch.*) The proctor's, the   25
lawyer's, the widow's, and [*starts*] at six? (*Aside.*) The
Ring? The Ring at six? Fiends! Who can say what may
happen? What, leave my father to perish? I'll not go!
Though all hell should brand me for a coward, I'll not go!
Mr. Smith, take care of my father! —Mark me, I recom-   30
mend my father to you!   *Exit.*

Enter Mr. Dornton.

DORNTON.

Where is Harry? Did not I hear his voice?

MR. SMITH.

He is this moment gone, sir.

12–13. I . . . marry!] *cancelled MS*;   *Ox.*
om. Inch.   22. Tol . . . wedding] *om. Q12.*
13. We'll marry] *om. Q12.*   24. does . . . me] *om. Q12.*
15.] *cancelled MS*; *om. Inch., Ox.*   26–27. The Ring? The Ring at
16–25. I have . . . son] *cancelled MS*;   six?] The Ring?—at six? *Ox.*
om. Inch.; knows what . . . son *om.*

18. *proctor*] clergyman.

–102–

DORNTON.

Gone where?

MR. SMITH.

Do you not suspect where, sir?   35

DORNTON (*alarmed*).

Suspect! What? Speak!

MR. SMITH.

To the widow Warren's.

DORNTON.

For what purpose?

MR. SMITH.

To marry her.

DORNTON.

Marry! The widow Warren!   40

MR. SMITH.

And save the house by her fortune.

DORNTON.

Generous Harry! Noble affectionate boy! I'd perish first!

MR. SMITH.

He seems very resolute. He has already had six thousand
pounds of her.

DORNTON.

Marry her? I shall go mad! —Where is Mr. Sulky?   45

MR. SMITH.

He is just returned. I hear him in the countinghouse.

DORNTON.

Tell him I wish to speak with him.   *Exit* Mr. Smith.
Harry Dornton and the widow Warren? I shall die in
Bedlam!

Enter Mr. Sulky.

Are we safe, Mr. Sulky?   50

SULKY.

For today, perhaps.

DORNTON.

What bank have we to begin tomorrow?

SULKY.

I can't tell. I fear not thirty thousand.

53. I can't ... thousand] Almost   fifteen thousand *MS.*
five—we shall have thirteen to

DORNTON.

> Mr. Sulky, you—you—have this day shown yourself an
> active partner, and a sincere friend.   55

SULKY.

> Humph.

DORNTON.

> I have long esteemed you; I esteem you more and more.

SULKY.

> Humph.

DORNTON (*hesitating*).

> My son Harry— You are a very good man, Mr. Sulky; a
> compassionate man, though you don't look so.   60

SULKY.

> Humph.

DORNTON.

> 'Tis pity to see so noble a youth—I am sure you would not
> wish him any harm, Mr. Sulky? I am sure you would not!

SULKY.

> Whom?

DORNTON.

> Harry Dornton. Would you? Would you? Would you,   65
> Mr. Sulky?

SULKY.

> A kind question.

DORNTON.

> Nay, I did not mean to be unkind, Mr. Sulky; you know I
> did not— Shall we not venture one step more to save him?

SULKY.

> Save? Impossible! Ruin only can reform him, total ruin.   70

DORNTON.

> You mistake, Mr. Sulky. His own misfortunes little affected
> him, but mine—! He is struck to the heart! —I know him!

SULKY.

> So do I.

DORNTON.

> Struck to the heart! I'm sure on't! He'll be a good man! A
> great man!   75

SULKY.

> Humph.

DORNTON.

You know the widow Warren, Mr. Sulky?

SULKY.

Don't you?

DORNTON.

I never saw her in my life. I hear she is full forty, her
manners absurd, her character cruel, and her morals—   80

SULKY.

Bad enough.

DORNTON.

Six thousand pounds at this moment is a great sum! I own
it! But do you think I ought not to venture?

SULKY.

Venture what?

DORNTON.

To—to take it from our bank?   85

SULKY.

For what?

DORNTON.

For—for the—the relief of Harry Dornton?

SULKY.

What you please! Take all! What is it to me?

DORNTON.

Nay, but, Mr. Sulky, you surely don't see the thing in the
right light?   90

SULKY.

I can starve, like the rest!

DORNTON (*snappish haste*).

Very well, Mr. Sulky! Very well! I perceive you can be
interested, and—and—!

SULKY.

And what?

DORNTON.

Very well, Mr. Sulky! Very well!   95

SULKY.

I can stare bankruptcy in the face as steadfastly as you can.

DORNTON.

Ay, ay! No doubt! The world is all alike! I am an old fool,
and so shall live and die!

SULKY.

> Why do you ask my advice? Take the money! Empty the
> coffers! Pour it all into his hat! Give him guineas to play at 100
> chuck farthing, and bank bills to curl his hair!

DORNTON.

> Very well, Mr. Sulky! —Friendship, generosity, a sense of
> justice? Oh! It's all a farce!

SULKY.

> Humph.

DORNTON (*rings*).

> Very well, sir! Very well!   105

Enter Servant.

> Is the carriage ready?

SERVANT.

> It's at the door, sir.   *Exit.*

DORNTON (*going, turns back*).

> So, Mr. Sulky, you could see him married to this widow, to
> whom you have so often as well as now given the worst of
> characters, rather than incur a little more risk for your 110
> friend?

SULKY.

> Marry?

DORNTON.

> Yes, marry!

SULKY.

> Whom?

DORNTON.

> The widow Warren, I tell you!   115

SULKY.

> And Harry Dornton?

DORNTON.

> Yes, and Harry Dornton!

SULKY.

> When? Where?

DORNTON.

> Immediately! With unexampled affection, to save me who
> am old and worthless, he would devote his youth, his great 120

---

101. *chuck farthing*] a gambling game of tossing coins.

qualities, and his noble heart, to all the torments which
such a marriage and such a woman can inflict!

SULKY.

Take the money!

DORNTON.

Are you serious, Mr. Sulky?

SULKY.

Take the money! Away! Begone! I would indeed starve, 125
inchmeal, rather than he should marry her!

DORNTON.

Mr. Sulky, you are a worthy man, a true friend!

SULKY.

Curse compliments! Make haste!   *Exeunt.*

ACT V

Scene, the Widow Warren's.
                    Sophia *and* Jenny *meeting.*

JENNY.

    So, miss! Here's your mamma just coming down.

SOPHIA (*much agitated*).

    Is she dressed?

JENNY.

    Oh, yes! I have decorationed her out like any king's coach
horse!

SOPHIA.

    It's very well.   5

JENNY.

    With her ribbands and ringlets stuck about and dangleating
down her back and all here—

SOPHIA.

    It's very well.

JENNY.

    Tight laced—Thomas called up to help.

SOPHIA.

    It's all very well! But it will be no wedding—   10

JENNY (*aside*).

    I hope not.

SOPHIA.

    He told her to her face that he loved me, and offered to give
her the money back. He'll never have her. And if he does
I don't care. I know I shall die brokenhearted, but I don't
care. I'll tell all to my dear grandma, for I'll not stay in this   15
wicked city. No! He shan't see me pine away. I know my
ghost will haunt him; but I can't help it. I never wished him
any harm, and had he but been truehearted and have
waited for me, I would—but it's no matter—he shan't see
a tear that I shed, nor hear the least sigh that I heave.   20

Enter the Widow Warren.

9. Thomas . . . help] *MS adds* —in   9.] *om. Ox.*
her white muslin chemise and pink   10. all very well] very well *Q12,*
sash!; *om. Inch.*   *Inch.*

JENNY (*looking, admiring, and walking round her*).

    Well, ma'am! I declare you're a picture!

WIDOW (*walking and surveying herself*).

    Do you think I look tolerably, Jenny? Shall I do execution?
    What is the matter, child?

SOPHIA.

    Mark my words, he'll never have you!

WIDOW.

    Poor thing!   25

SOPHIA.

    He never will!   *Knocking heard at the street door.*

WIDOW.

    Run, Jenny, see who it is!   *Exit* Jenny.
    Go up to your chamber, child.

SOPHIA.

    No! I will stay here.

WIDOW.

    Begone to your chamber, I say, miss!   30

SOPHIA.

    Beat me if you please, kill me, but I will not!

Re-enter Jenny.

JENNY.

    Here's an elderly gentleman, ma'am, asks to speak to you.

WIDOW.

    Will you begone, miss?

SOPHIA.

    Since it is not he I don't want to stay. I only want to look
    him in the face once more.   *Exit.*   35

WIDOW.

    How is he dressed?

JENNY.

    In grey, ma'am.

WIDOW (*considering*).

    In grey?

JENNY.

    Yes, ma'am.

38. grey?] grey! *Q 9–12.*

WIDOW (*hoping*).

    In dark grey? 40

JENNY.

    Yes, ma'am.

WIDOW (*earnestly*).

    Does he look like a parson, Jenny?

JENNY.

    Why, ma'am, he is a soberly, smug, jobation-looking man enough.

WIDOW.

    Let him be shown in. I dare say it is the divine. 45

Footman introduces Mr. Dornton.

DORNTON.

    Your humble servant, madam.

WIDOW (*with great respect*).

    Sir, your very most humble servant.

DORNTON.

    I presume you are unacquainted with me?

WIDOW (*simpering*).

    I believe I can penetrate, sir.

DORNTON.

    Can you, madam? 50

WIDOW (*with her fan before her face*).

    You—you come on the—part of—young Mr. Dornton?

DORNTON (*surprised*).

    I do!

WIDOW (*aside*).

    It is the parson! —Would you be so indulgent as to be seated, sir?

DORNTON.

    Excuse me, madam. 55

WIDOW.

    Would you be pleased to take any refreshment, sir?

44–45. enough . . . Let him] enough to be sure, but then he has got his hair tied. WIDOW. Oh, that is beginning to be the fashion among your spruce cauliflower clergymen, Jenny. Let him *MS*.

---

43. *jobation-looking*] severe, reproving.

DORNTON.

Madam! None, I thank you.

WIDOW.

A morsel of seedcake, a French biscuit, a bit of orange loaf,
a glass of Constantia, or a jelly? I know these little cordial
comforts are agreeable consolations to gentlemen of your   60
cloth.

DORNTON (*surveying himself*).

Cloth!

WIDOW.

No offense, I hope? I participate in them myself.

DORNTON.

Hem! No doubt!

WIDOW.

You are acquainted with Mr. Dornton?   65

DORNTON.

Why—yes—I am I believe one of his oldest acquaintance.

WIDOW.

Then I dare say you have a great regard for him?

DORNTON.

Hem! Yes, I—had a—sort of a friendship for him even
before he was born.

WIDOW.

Sir! Oh! You are intimate with the family?   70

DORNTON.

Yes—yes, madam!

WIDOW.

And know his father?

DORNTON (*shrugs*).

Um— Why—though I have kept him company from the
day of his birth to this very hour, they tell me I don't know
him yet!   75

WIDOW.

Ay, indeed! Is he so odd?

DORNTON.

Sometimes. To my great regret I have sometimes found him
a very absurd old gentleman!

---

59. *Constantia*] a wine, both red and white, produced near Cape Town,
South Africa.

WIDOW.

> I am sorry for it! Because as I am soon to become— hymeneally—his intimate—relation—I—I—! 80

Maidenly affectation.

DORNTON.

> You would wish for a sensible indulgent—papa— *Smiles.*

WIDOW (*simpering*).

> It's natural, sir.

DORNTON.

> Ha! I dare not say too much in his favor.

WIDOW (*nodding very significantly*).

> Nay, though I have a vast—hum—ha—regard for young Mr. Dornton—I own I have no great predilection of 85 opinion for the father!

DORNTON (*suddenly*).

> Nor he for you, madam!

WIDOW.

> Do you think so?

DORNTON.

> I am sure so!

WIDOW.

> I warrant, sir, he is, as you say, a very precise acrimonious 90 person! A tetchy repugnant kind of old gentleman!

DORNTON.

> I said no such thing, madam!

WIDOW.

> Ah! A little caution, sir, to be sure, becomes gentlemen of your cloth.

DORNTON.

> Cloth again! I don't know what you mean by my cloth, but 95 Mr. Dornton, madam, is little older than yourself; nor does he think himself half so repugnant.

WIDOW.

> Sir!

DORNTON (*recollecting himself*).

> Madam! I—I beg your pardon! I— *Bowing.*

Knocking heard.

91. gentleman] scarecrow *Q12*; A
. . . gentleman *om. Ox.*

WIDOW (*enraptured*).

Oh! Here I dare say comes the bridegroom!   100

Crosses to the door.

DORNTON (*aside*).

My curst vivacity! I can never tell her after this who I am.

Walks up the stage.

Enter Harry Dornton, *in haste.*

WIDOW.

Oh, you rover!

HARRY.

Well, my kind widow! (Mr. Dornton *turns quick round at hearing his son's voice, and gradually approaches.*) My loving compassionate widow! I am come posthaste to cast myself 105 once more on your bounty!

WIDOW.

Hush!

HARRY.

To entreat instant commiseration, and aid!

WIDOW (*aloud*).

Hem! Hem!

HARRY.

I have not a minute to spare!   110

WIDOW (*whisper*).

He's here! He's come! A waspish, tetchy—! Hem! (*Aloud.*) Your friend has been here some time, Mr. Dornton!

HARRY.

My friend! What friend?

WIDOW (*pointing to Mr. Dornton*).

Your friend the clergyman.

HARRY.

Clergyman! —You— (*Turning, sees his father at his elbow.*) 115 My father!

WIDOW.

His father!   *Pause.*

DORNTON.

Well, Harry, why do you look so blank? I am glad you are

100. dare say comes] dare comes *Q 4–6.*   100. bridegroom!] bridegroom in smiling supererogation of haste! *MS.*

here. Your coming, and the mutual sincerity with which
this lady and I have just spoken our sentiments, will save all 120
circumlocution. At present we understand each other.

WIDOW.

Sir—I—

DORNTON.

Oh, madam, never retract. Let us continue the like plain
honest dealing.

WIDOW.

But—sir—Mr. Dornton's affection—   125

DORNTON.

Ha, ha, ha! Affection, madam!   *Pitying her delusion.*

HARRY.

Sir—

DORNTON.

Harry! I know your motives! Will never forget them! But
the cause of them has ceased.

HARRY.

Sir? —Beware! No false compassion! Remember not the 130
vile reprobate that was your son! I spurn at existence that
is coupled with your misery!

DORNTON.

Harry! Our danger is over.

HARRY.

Are you—are you serious?

DORNTON.

Mr. Sulky is a worthy man! His rich uncle is dead, and has 135
left him sole heir. Our books too have been examined, and
exceed our best hopes.

HARRY.

Tol de rol—!

DORNTON.

Here is your money, madam.

HARRY.

My father saved—? Tol de rol—!   140

WIDOW (*ready to cry*).

Nay, but—Mr. Dornton! Sir!

130. Sir] Sir! *Inch., Ox.*   138. Tol de rol] My— *Ox.*

DORNTON.

I must beg you will take it.

HARRY.

Rejoice, widow! Rejoice! Sing, shout! Tol de rol!

WIDOW (*whimpering restrained*).

I do not want the money, sir! Filthy money! And as to what
I said, though you have arrested Mr. Milford—   145

HARRY.

Ha!   *Starts, considers, and looks at his watch.*

WIDOW.

I am sorry. I beg your pardon. And if Mr. Dornton—

DORNTON.

Why don't you speak, Harry? Where are you going?

                    Harry Dornton *crosses hastily to the door.*

Come back, Harry! Stay, I say!

HARRY.

I cannot stay! I must fly! My honor is at stake!   *Exit.*   150

DORNTON (*alarmed*).

His honor! His honor at stake! —Here, here, madam!
                    Offering her bankbills.

WIDOW.

Nay, sir—

DORNTON.

'Sdeath, madam, take your money.   *Exit.*

WIDOW.

Cruel—usage! Faithless—men—blind—stupid! I'll forsake
and forswear the whole sex!   155

    Enter Jenny *with glee on tiptoe, as if she had been on the watch.*

JENNY.

Ma'am.

WIDOW (*sobbing*).

Savage race!

JENNY.

Ma'am! Ma'am! Mr. Goldfinch, ma'am!

WIDOW (*brightens up*).

Hey! Mr. Goldfinch? Was that what you said, Jenny?
Where?   160

144. I . . . sir] *cancelled MS.*   156.] *om. Ox.*

JENNY.

Below, ma'am. I persuaded him to come up, but he is quite surly.

WIDOW.

Oh! He is coming? Well! I think I will see him. Yes, I think I will.

JENNY.

I always told you, ma'am, Mr. Goldfinch for me.   165

WIDOW.

Did you?

JENNY.

But he says he will have your written promise this very night, or never speak to you more. I hear him. (*Adjusting the widow's dress.*) Law, ma'am, you had better give a few touches—hereabout! Your eyes will have double the spirit 170 and fire.

WIDOW.

Will they?   *Exit.*

Enter Goldfinch.

GOLDFINCH.

Where's the dowager?

JENNY.

Hush! Mind what I said to you. It is too late now for a license, so be sure get the promise. Don't flinch!   175

GOLDFINCH.

Me flinch? Game to the backbone!

JENNY.

Hush!

Re-enter the Widow Warren.

GOLDFINCH.

Here I am once more, widow.

WIDOW.

Ah, rambler!

GOLDFINCH.

Are you cured of the tantarums?   180

WIDOW.

Nay, Mr. Goldfinch!

GOLDFINCH.

Must I keep my distance?

WIDOW.

Unkind!

GOLDFINCH.

Am I a gentleman now?

WIDOW.

Killing!   185

GOLDFINCH.

Look you, widow, I know your tricks. Skittish! Won't
answer the whip! Run out of the course! Take the rest!
—So give me your promise.

WIDOW.

My promise!

GOLDFINCH.

Signed and sealed.   190

WIDOW.

Naughty man. You shan't—I won't let you tyrannize over
a palpitating heart!

GOLDFINCH.

Palpi—   (*To* Jenny.)   What does she say?

WIDOW.

You shan't steal on hymeneal transports!

GOLDFINCH.

What's that?   195

WIDOW.

Connubial ecstasies!

GOLDFINCH.

Nu—what?

WIDOW.

Go, intruder!

GOLDFINCH.

Oh! What, you won't?

WIDOW.

I'll never forgive you.   200

GOLDFINCH.

I'm off.

194–197.] *om. Ox.*

-117-

WIDOW.

Cruel man!

GOLDFINCH.

I'm off.

WIDOW (*calling*).

Mr. Goldfinch!

GOLDFINCH.

I'm off— 205

WIDOW.

You shall have the promise!

GOLDFINCH.

Oh, ho! Why, then I pull up.

WIDOW.

Barbarous youth! Could you leave me? —But I must send to Mr. Silky.

GOLDFINCH.

No, no! Let me have the promise directly! I'll go myself to 210 Silky.

WIDOW.

Will you, Mr. Goldfinch?

GOLDFINCH.

Will I not? Take a hack, mount the box—hayait! Scud away for the old scoundrel! I'm a deep one! Know the course every inch! I'm the lad for a widow! That's your sort! 215

WIDOW.

Saucy man! I'll be very angry with you.

GOLDFINCH.

Soon be back!

WIDOW.

Adieu! Fly swiftly, ye minutes!

GOLDFINCH.

But I must have the promise first!

WIDOW.

I will go and write it. Come, dissembler, come! 220

Exit languishing.

GOLDFINCH.

She's an old courser! But I knew I should take her at the double!

Enter Milford.

208. youth] man *MS.*

MILFORD.

So, Charles, where's the widow?

GOLDFINCH.

The widow's mine!

MILFORD.

Yours?   225

GOLDFINCH.

I'm the lad! All's concluded. Going post for old Silky.

Offers to go at every speech, but is eagerly stopped by Milford.

MILFORD.

Silky, did you say?

GOLDFINCH.

Am to pay the miserly rascal fifty thousand pounds down!
But mum! That's a secret!

MILFORD.

You are raving!   230

GOLDFINCH.

Tellee he has her on the hip! She can't marry without his
consent!

MILFORD.

But why?

GOLDFINCH.

Don't know. The close old rogue won't tell. Has got some
deed, he says—some writing.   235

MILFORD.

Indeed!

GOLDFINCH.

Yes. But it's all hush! I shall be a higher fellow than ever,
Jack! Go to the second spring meeting—take you with me—
come down a few to the sweaters and trainers—the knowing
ones—the lads. Get into the secret. Lay it on thick. Seven 240
hundred to five favorite against the field! Done! I'll do it
again! Done! Five times over ditto repeated! Done, done!
Off they go! Winner lays by—pretends to want foot—odds
rise high! Take 'em—winner whispered lame—lags after—
odds higher and higher! Take 'em—creeps up—breathes 245
'em over the flat—works 'em up hill—passes the distance

237. it's all hush] it's a secret *MS,*   241. favorite] Meteor *MS.*
Inch., Ox.

post—still only second—betting chair in an uproar! Neck to
neck! Lets him out—shows him the whip—shoots by like an
arrow! Oh, dammee a hollow thing! That's your sort!   *Exit.*

MILFORD.

Fifty thousand to Silky for his consent because of some deed,   250
some writing? —If it should be the—? It must! By heaven,
it must!   *Exit hastily.*

[V.ii]   *Scene changes to the Ring in Hyde Park.*
             Harry Dornton looking at his watch.

HARRY.

How long must I wait? I see nothing of Milford. I'll cut off
that bailiff's ears if he have betrayed me.   *Walks about.*

Enter Mr. Dornton *out of breath.*

DORNTON.

So, Harry!

HARRY.

My father again!

DORNTON (*panting*).

What do you do here, Harry?   5

HARRY.

Sir—I—I want air.

DORNTON.

So do I. A pretty dance you have led me. What brought you
hither?   (*Sudden recollection.*)   Where's the money you had
of the widow?   (*Pause, seeming to dread an answer.*)   Where
is the money, Harry?   10

HARRY (*reluctantly*).

Gone, sir.

DORNTON.

Gone!

HARRY.

Most of it.

249. thing! That's] thing! All my
eye! That's *MS.*
250. deed] instrument *MS, Inch.,*
Ox.

251. be the—] be the will *Q12.*
[V.ii]
4. again!] again? *Q9–11, Inch.;*
again. *Ox.*

DORNTON.

> And your creditors not paid? (*Another pause.*) And your
> creditors not paid? 15

HARRY.

> No, sir.

DORNTON (*raises his hands*).

> I suspected—I foreboded this!

> Harry Dornton *walks up the stage.*

> He has been at some gaming house, lost all, quarreled, and
> come here to put a miserable end to a miserable existence!
> Oh, who would be a father! *Extreme anguish.* 20

> *Enter* Waiter.

WAITER.

> I am sent on an April day kind of errand here. I think this
> is what they call the Ring. (*Looks round.*) Hey! Who is
> this? (*Surveying* Mr. Dornton.) Pray, sir, is your name
> Dornton?

DORNTON.

> It is. 25

WAITER.

> Then I am right. Mr. Milford, sir, has sent me with this
> note.

HARRY (*advancing*).

> It is for me, sir!

DORNTON.

> How do you know, Harry?

HARRY.

> Sir, I am certain! I must beg—! 30

DORNTON.

> This is no time for ceremony! (*Reads.*) "Dear Harry,
> forgive the provocation I have given you; forget the wrong
> I have done your father—" Me!— "I will submit to any
> disgrace rather than lift my hand against your life. I would
> have come and apologized even on my knees, but am 35
> prevented. J. Milford."

> *Stands a moment crumpling up the letter.*

21–23. I . . . this?] *om. Ox.*

---

21. *April . . . errand*] practical joke.

Why, Harry! What? What is this? Tell me—tell me—is it
in paying Milford's debts you have expended the money?

HARRY.

It is, sir.

DORNTON (*after raising his clasped hands in rapture as if to return thanks,
suddenly suppresses his feelings*).

But how had he wronged me? Why did you come here to   40
fight him?

HARRY.

Sir—he—he spoke disrespectfully of you.   *Pause.*

DORNTON (*with his eyes fixed on his son, till unable any longer to contain
himself he covers them with one hand and stretches out the other*).

Harry!

HARRY (*taking his father's hand, but turning his back likewise to conceal his
agitation*).

My father!   *Pause.*

DORNTON (*struggling affection*).

Harry! Harry!   *Pause.*   45

HARRY.

Dear sir, let us fly to console poor Milford!

DORNTON.

What you will, Harry! Do with me what you will. Oh, who
would not be a father!   *Exeunt.*

[V.iii]   *Scene changes to the house of the Widow Warren.*
                    Enter Milford *and* Mr. Sulky.

MILFORD.

The fool Goldfinch himself informed me, sir, that Silky is to
receive fifty thousand pounds for his consent!

SULKY.

Fifty thousand! Zounds! Why, then the old scoundrel must
have got possession of the will.

MILFORD.

Which is indubitably meant to be destroyed. Goldfinch is   5
just returned with Silky. They are now with the widow, all
in high glee, and are coming up here immediately, no
doubt to settle the business in private.

SULKY.

What can be done?

MILFORD.

We must hide ourselves somewhere, and spring upon them.   10

SULKY.

I hate hiding! It's deceit, and deceit is the resource of a
rascal.

MILFORD.

But there is no avoiding it! We cannot get legal assistance in
time! Here are two closets! Do you go into one, and I'll shut
myself up in the other. We shall hear what they are about,   15
and can burst upon them at the proper moment.

SULKY.

Well, if it must be so. But it's a vile, paltry refuge!

MILFORD.

I hear them coming! Make haste!

> *Exeunt* Sulky *and* Milford *into the closets.*

Enter Silky, Widow, *and* Goldfinch.

SILKY.

Ha, ha, ha! I told you, madam, I should hear from you
when you wanted me! I knew it must come to that! But you   20
are a lucky man, Mr. Goldfinch, and I'm a lucky man; ay,
and you are a lucky woman too, madam! We are all in luck!

GOLDFINCH.

Ay, dammee, old one, you have been concerned in many a
good thing in your time!

SILKY.

Ah, ha, ha, ha, ha! To be sure I have! I must provide for my   25
family, Mr. Goldfinch!

WIDOW.

It is indeed a fortunate event! Do you not participate my
raptures, Mr. Goldfinch?

GOLDFINCH.

To be sure. It's a deep scheme! It's knowing a thing or two!
Hey, old one? Pigeoning the greenhorns!   30

SILKY.

All so safe too, so snug! I am so pleased, and so happy! It's
all our own! Not a soul will know of it but our three selves!

GOLDFINCH.

Oh, yes. One more, old one—

SILKY (*alarmed*).

　　Ay! Who? Who?

GOLDFINCH.

　　Your father—Beelzebub!　　　　　　　　　　　　　35

SILKY.

　　Lord! Mr. Goldfinch, don't terrify me!

WIDOW.

　　To be sure, it must be owned you are a shocking old rogue,
　　Mr. Silky! But there is no doing without you. So make haste
　　with your deeds and your extortions; for really we should
　　be very glad to be rid of your company.　　　　　　40

SILKY.

　　Well, well, I'm ready—I'll not long interrupt your amorous
　　haste. I am a man of business! I expected how it would be,
　　and have a legal instrument here, ready drawn up by my
　　own hand, which, when it is signed and sealed, will make all
　　safe!　　　　　　　　　　　　　　　　　　　45

WIDOW.

　　But where is the will?

SILKY.

　　Oh, I have it. First however let us be secure.

*Locks both the chamber doors; is going to read, but looks round, sees the closet
doors, and with great anxiety and cunning locks them too.*

GOLDFINCH.

　　You're an old trader in sin! There's no being too deep for
　　you!

SILKY.

　　Ah, ha, ha, ha! Do you think so, Mr. Goldfinch?　　　50

GOLDFINCH.

　　But I should like to see you on your deathbed!

　　　　　　　　　　　　　A blow from one of the closets.

SILKY.

　　Bless my soul! What's that?

GOLDFINCH.

　　Zounds! Odd enough! I believe he's coming for you before
　　your time!

42. haste. I] haste. WIDOW. Do　　Odious being! Profane not　the
you hear, Mr. Goldfinch? Amorous!　　tender epithet! SILKY. I *MS.*

WIDOW.

    It was very strange! 55

SILKY.

    I declare I am all of a tremble!

WIDOW.

    Come, come, let us get the shocking business over! Where is
the will?

GOLDFINCH.

    Don't shake so, man!

SILKY.

    Well, well! —First sign the bond! 60
               Widow and Goldfinch *going to sign, another knock heard.*
    Lord have mercy upon me!

GOLDFINCH.

    I smell sulphur!

WIDOW.

    Save me, Mr. Goldfinch!

SILKY.

    The candles burn blue! *Pause.*

GOLDFINCH.

    Pshaw! Zounds, it's only some cat in the closet! 65

SILKY.

    I heard it in both the closets!

GOLDFINCH.

    Why, then there are two cats! —Come! I'll sign—
               Widow and Goldfinch *sign the bond.*

SILKY.

    Where's the promise.

GOLDFINCH (*laying it on the table*).

    Here it is!

SILKY.

    And here is the will, which, that all may be safe, we will 70
immediately commit to the flames.

*Is going to burn it at the candle. Four successive loud knocks are heard, one
from each of the doors. Silky starts, drops one candle, and overturns the other.
The stage dark.*

---

59. shake] skake *Q 9–11.*   FINCH. Ay do, and defy the devil!
71.] *After l. 71, MS prints:* GOLD-

Lord have mercy upon us!

GOLDFINCH.

My hair stands an end!

> *Violent knocking at both closets and at the doors.*

WIDOW.

Save me, Mr. Goldfinch! Protect me! Ah!   *Shrieks.*

Sulky *and* Milford *burst open the closets and seize on the bond and promise, then open the chamber doors, at one of which enter* Jenny *with lights, and at the other* Sophia, Harry Dornton, *and* Mr. Dornton.

SOPHIA.

Dear, ma, what's the matter?   75

SULKY.

Where is the will?

> Silky *recovers himself and snatches it up.*

Give it me, you old scoundrel! Give it me this instant, or I'll throttle you!   *Wrests it from him.*

MILFORD.

So, gentlemen! You are a pretty pair of knaves!

SULKY.

And you are a very worthy lady!   80

WIDOW.

Don't talk to me, man! Don't talk to me! I shall never recover my senses again!

HARRY.

What has happened, gentlemen? How came you thus all locked up together?

DORNTON.

Are you here, Mr. Silky?   85

SULKY.

Yes! There's the honest, grateful, friendly Mr. Silky! Who would betray his friends, plunder the living, and defraud the dead, for the ease of his conscience, and to provide for his family!

GOLDFINCH.

Old one! You're done up!   90

SULKY.

And here is the girlish old coquette, who would rob her

daughter and leave her husband's son to rot in a dungeon,
that she might marry the first fool she could find!

GOLDFINCH.

Widow! You are dished!

        Sulky *examines the will.*

Lost your last chance!   95

DORNTON.

A broken gamester, nurtured in idleness, ignorance, and
dissipation, whose ridings, racings, and drivings are over, and
whose whole train of horses, dogs, curricles, phaetons, and
fooleries must come to the hammer immediately, is no great
loss.   100

SOPHIA.

ꞌ   Oh, la! And what is coming to the hammer?

DORNTON.

Oh, the hammer is an instrument by which Folly is publicly
knocked down to the best bidder, after which she rises,
gambols, whisks away, makes a short flying tour, and
gallops back to be publicly knocked down again.   105

SOPHIA.

Dear! Poor Mr. Goldfinch!

DORNTON.

I knew your father, sir; 'tis happy for him that he is dead!
If you will forsake these courses and apply to trade—

GOLDFINCH.

Damn trade! Who's for the spring meeting? Cross 'em and
wind 'em! Seven to five you don't name the winner! I'm for 110
life and a curricle! A cut at the caster, and the long odds!
Damn trade! The four aces, a back hand, and a lucky nick!
I'm a deep one! That's your sort!   *Exit.*

SULKY.

And now, madam—

WIDOW.

Keep off, monster! You smell of malice, cruelty, and 115
persecution!

---

95. last chance] chance *MS.*   *Q 12, Ox.*
101–106. And . . . Goldfinch] *om.*   101–106.] *om. Inch.*

  94. *dished*] ruined.
  99. *come to the hammer*] be sold at auction.
  109–112. *Cross . . . nick*] contemporary gambling terms.

SULKY.

No, madam; I smell of honesty! A drug you nauseate, but
with which you must forcibly be dosed; I have glanced over
the will, and find I have the power.

WIDOW.

Let me go, goblin! You are a hideous person, and I hate the 120
sight of you! Your breast is flint! Flint! Unfeeling Gorgon,
and I abominate you!   *Exit into an inner chamber.*

SOPHIA.

Nah, you are a kind, good, cross old soul; and I am sure you
will forgive my poor ma! We ought all to forget and
forgive! Ought not we, Mr. Dornton?   125

HARRY (*with rapture, and looking to his father*).

Do you hear her, sir?

DORNTON.

Harry has told me of your innocent, pure, and unsuspecting
heart. I love you for having called me an ugly monster!

SOPHIA (*to* Harry).

La, Mr. Dornton, how could you—!

SULKY.

Harry, give me your hand. You have a generous and a 130
noble nature. But your generosity would have proved more
pernicious than even your dissipation. No misfortunes, no,
not the beggary and ruin of a father, could justify so unprincipled a marriage!

DORNTON (*to* Mr. Sulky).

And now my friend!   135

MILFORD.

My father!

HARRY.

My—!

SULKY.

Whoo! If you wish to get another word from me tonight,
have done.   (*Turning to* Silky.)   I hate fawning!

SILKY.

Ah, Mr. Sulky, you will have your humor.   140

SULKY.

The undiscriminating generosity of this young man sup-
ported you in your day of distress; for which, serpentlike,
you turned to sting your preserver.

SILKY.

Ah, you will have your humor.

SULKY.

Yes; and it is my humor to see that your villainy shall be 145
exposed in its true colors. Hypocrisy, falsehood, and fraud
are your familiars. To screen your avarice, you made it be-
lieved that this gentleman had been the cause of lodging the
detainers, and had done the dirty work of which even you
were ashamed. But the creditors shall receive their full 150
demand.

DORNTON.

The proposal is just. Listen to that worthy man; and if you
can, be honest with a good grace. Everything will then be
readily adjusted, and I hope to the satisfaction of all parties.

Exeunt Omnes.

EPILOGUE

Spoken by Mrs. Mattocks

My scenic faults and follies laid aside,
No widow now, nor disappointed bride,
My own plain self I once again resume;
Sent by the author here, to know his doom.
Would you condemn him? Do, with all my heart.   5
To own the truth, I don't half like my part:
Through five long acts the butt of ridicule,⎞
A hard unfeeling heart, a flirt, a fool,   ⎬
My daughter's tyrant and my lover's tool,   ⎠
I hoped the bitter pill he'd overcome,   10
By making up an epilogue sugarplum.
But no! —Madam, said he, take my advice,   ⎞
And conquer feelings which are much too nice: ⎬
Fear not to hold the mirror up to vice.   ⎠
We, who paint human characters, must show them   15
Such as they are; or nobody would know them.
—But, sir, the sex! A woman! —Very true:
I'm sorry so many sat for me, while I drew.
—Sure! Really, sir! —Nay, don't be angry, madam:
Both ate the apple, Eve as well as Adam.   20
And, while through thick and thin the passions goad,
Nor Eve nor Adam stay to pick their road.
And, as for epilogue, I'll not descend
Bad play by worse buffoonery to mend.
—Mister, said I, you are too wise by half;   25
Folks don't come here to learn, they come to laugh:
And, if they choose like Hottentots their meat,
You must provide them what they please to eat.
Lord, sir! The beauties of proportion never please
Such as delight in frippery and frieze!   30
Do we not see, by man of travel'd taste
In open hall on rising pillar plac'd,
Griffon or sphinx th' insulted eye before,

*Epilogue om. Q12, Inch.; lines in MS.
arranged 1–28, 35–40, 29–34, 41–46*

While Plato's bust stands hid behind the door?
But good advice I find is thrown away!   35
—Yes, good advice is like a rainy day,
Which, though it make our barns and coffers full,
Is often splenetic, and always dull.
Our common cause, then, let us fairly trust
With those who are to sense and nature just.   40

To the audience.

The richest soil, and most invig'rate seed,
Will here and there infested be with weed:
The gaudy poppy rears its broad bull head
Among the wheat, somnif'rous dews to shed:
Then, wheresoe'er rank couch grass, fern, or tares are   45
    found,
'Tis yours to handweed, horsehoe, clear, and till the
    ground.

FINIS

Appendix A

Lines Omitted in Representation

Below are listed those lines in *The Road to Ruin* which were not spoken on the stage in the first production. Q1 through Q11 set off these lines with quotation marks. Q12 prints the lines without quotation marks and without any statement that they were omitted in representation. Mrs. Inchbald and W. Oxberry generally, although not invariably, omit them; and the MS occasionally cancels them (see textual notes).

[I.i]
  115–118. Where . . . blacklegs!
[I.iii]
  41–45. What! . . . host.
  260–266. That's . . . Heigho!
[II.i]
  10–12. and she . . . clothes!
  272–275. if I . . . indeed
[III.i]
  118–120. To imagine . . . year!
  132–134. Was taken . . . week.
  265–268. You have . . . byways—
[III.ii]
  11–14. the unnatural . . . loathsomeness!
  17. Yes . . . it!
[IV.i]
  6–12. Goddess! . . . tol de rol.
  18–27. Fie . . . begin!
  47–55. Elegant . . . though—!
  61–65. Will he? Words . . . choice.
  81–99. —he shall . . . saved?
  103–104. No . . . Else
  110–116. Thou art . . . Pactolus!

122–124. My father's! My pocket . . . cast.

133–134. Thou brazen . . . occupation!

134–135. I have not got rid of the old lady!

137–138. Before . . . decreed!

141. An't you a sad man?

142–144. Thou shalt . . . traffic thine!

149. You . . . man!

157. I'll . . . ever.

172–173. and everybody . . . you;

207. Tonight, you know, Mr. Dornton—?

244–250. What's . . . sort!

[IV.ii]

21–24. Pshaw . . . tomorrow.

29. Why . . . that!

31. I must . . . tonight—

[IV.iii]

12–13. I will . . . marry!

15–25. Will . . . son?

[V.i]

9. Thomas . . . help.

[V.iii]

101–106. And . . . Goldfinch!

[Epilogue]

41–46. The . . . ground.

Appendix B

Chronology

1745	Thomas Holcroft born in Orange Court, London, December 10.
1751	Holcroft's father, failing in business, moved to the country, where Holcroft peddled with him.
1757	Holcroft apprenticed as stableboy at Newmarket.
1760	Worked as apprentice shoemaker with father in London.
1764	Taught in a Liverpool school.
1765	Contributions in the *Whitehall Evening Post*.
1770–71	In Dublin with Charles Macklin as actor and prompter.
1771–77	Strolling player in England with the Kembles' company and other companies.
1778	Employed in London by Sheridan in minor parts. First play, *The Crisis*, performed once at Drury Lane.
1780	First novel, *Alwyn*.
1781	First comedy, *Duplicity*, produced at Covent Garden; quitted the stage for literature.
1783	In Paris, April–October, as correspondent of *Morning Herald*.
1784	His pirated version of *Le Mariage de Figaro* produced at Covent Garden, Holcroft appearing as Figaro.
1786	Met William Godwin.
1792	*The Road to Ruin* produced at Covent Garden February 18, with 37 performances during the first season. Novel, *Anna St. Ives*, published.
1794	In October indicted for high treason with Thomas Hardy, Horne Tooke, John Thelwall and others. Released in December without trial or pardon.
1794–97	Published *Hugh Trevor*.
1799	Married his fourth wife, Louisa Mercier. In financial difficulties; sold his library and pictures and moved to Hamburg.

1802	Returned to London. In November *A Tale of Mystery*, considered the first British melodrama, produced at Covent Garden.
1807	Again in financial difficulties.
1809	Died, March 23, after a long illness, in poverty. Buried in Marylebone cemetery, London. His widow later married James Kenney, the dramatist and friend of Charles Lamb.

1⁵0 1 4329